DEVELOPMENT AND DIGNITY

The first 15 years of the
Inter-American Foundation

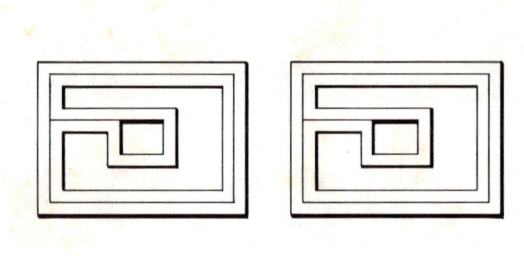

DEVELOPMENT AND DIGNITY

Grassroots Development and the Inter-American Foundation

PATRICK BRESLIN

INTER-AMERICAN FOUNDATION   Rosslyn, Virginia

DEVELOPMENT AND DIGNITY

INTER-AMERICAN FOUNDATION
Rosslyn, Virginia

Published in 1987 in the United States of America by the Inter-American Foundation, 1515 Wilson Blvd., Rosslyn, Virginia 22209. The material in this publication is in the public domain and may be reprinted freely without written permission of the author or publisher.

Library of Congress Cataloguing-in-Publication Data
Main entry under title:
  Development and Dignity
  1. Inter-American Foundation—History. 2. Economic assistance, American—Latin America—History.
I. Inter-American Foundation. II. Title.
HC125.B725 1987   338.91'7308'0601   87-3920
ISBN 0-8133-0538-1

Printed and bound in the United States of America by Westview Press, Inc., Frederick A. Praeger, Publisher, 5500 Central Avenue, Boulder, Colorado 80301. The paper used in this publication meets the minimum requirements of the American National Standard for Permanence of Paper for Printed Library Materials Z39.48-1984.

For Cathleen and Glenna

Photographs

Cover: *Family tending a community onion plot in San Juan de Kadarony, Bolivia. (Mitchell Denburg)*

Chapter 1: *Peasants attending a meeting in Ecuadorean highlands. (Sean Sprague)*

Chapter 2: *Migrant workers build their own homes in Cartago, Colombia. (Mitchell Denburg)*

Chapter 3: *Mapuche Indian woman near Temuco, in Southern Chile. (Marcelo Montecino)*

Chapter 4: *Peasant farmers in Ecuador returning home from their fields. (Sean Sprague)*

Chapter 5: *Shantytown in Guayaquil, Ecuador. (Sean Sprague)*

Chapter 6: *Mourners at funeral of Chilean poet Pablo Neruda. (Marcelo Montecino)*

Chapter 7: *Cooperative meeting in the Dominican Republic. (Stephen Vetter)*

Chapter 8: *Leaders of a Mataco Indian community in El Sausalito, Argentina. (Miguel Sayago)*

Contents

Preface and Acknowledgements ... ix

PROLOGUE ... xi

PART ONE: AN EXPERIMENT

    1 The Foundation Is Launched ... 4

    2 Southern Winds Fill the Sails ... 18

PART TWO: PRESERVATION AND CHANGE

    3 A Sense of Identity ... 28

    4 The Troubled Countryside ... 40

    5 Coping with the Cities ... 56

    6 Islands of Democracy ... 78

PART THREE: THE FOUNDATION'S NICHE

    7 A Prophetic Institution ... 92

    8 Development and Dignity ... 106

Preface and Acknowledgements

EVERY FIVE YEARS or so, the Inter-American Foundation feels the need to take a look at itself and its work in Latin America and the Caribbean, hoping that its experience will be helpful to others interested in development. Last year was the Foundation's fifteenth anniversary, and this is the third such book-length overview. The first was *They Know How* (1976), the second, *In Partnership With People* (1984). Having written several previous articles for the Foundation, I was familiar with the kinds of people that the Foundation tended to support. Rereading *They Know How*, which lays out the Foundation's rationale for grassroots projects, I was struck by the Appendix, which contains a sample of reactions to the book by grantees. It was clear from their comments that these people regarded the Foundation as an important experiment in cooperation between the United States and its neighbors in the hemisphere, that they had a great deal of affection for the Foundation, and that they felt entitled to express their opinions about it quite openly and bluntly. If I could find more people like that, I thought, I could write about the Foundation through their eyes.

For the next several months, I crisscrossed the region, meeting with over a hundred Foundation grantees, current and past. I also interviewed people who weren't grantees, but had observed the Foundation's approach: journalists, academics, government officials, human rights activists, development workers, even, once, the inevitable cab driver after we were rear-ended on a Kingston thoroughfare. To fill the time before the police arrived, I asked him for his thoughts on women working in the construction industry, a project the Foundation was then supporting.

I also interviewed Foundation representatives, a band of distinct individuals who have a common commitment to and great respect for the poor people of the hemisphere; and the Foundation's support staff who manage to express that same commitment and respect in their daily work even though they are seldom able, unlike the representatives, to meet grantees in person and see their projects in action.

There were many, many more people who helped by sharing their memories and their insights: former staff members, former presidents, former board members. Others helped with the book itself: Deborah Szekely, the current president, whose idea it was; Sheldon Annis, the former publications director, who helped me get the project going;

Scott Kuster, who did so much of the early research; Kathryn Shaw, the current publications officer, and Diane Bendahmane, my editor.

I'm grateful to them all for their interest and support and encouragement. But I'm especially grateful to the people all over the hemisphere who talked to me about their work for development and a better future for their societies. I think the book is an accurate reflection of how they see the Inter-American Foundation. If it is not, I shall surely hear from them.

Patrick Breslin
April 1987

Prologue

ABOUT EIGHT YEARS AGO, somewhere between Asunción, Paraguay, and the Brazilian border, I came across the worst development project I have ever seen. In company with five or six foreign assistance experts, I visited a farmer participating in a program to improve cattle stock. The visit had been arranged beforehand and the farmer was awaiting us, dressed in pants tied rather than belted over his paunch, a white shirt, sandals. He rolled a straw hat in his hands. A few yards away, a knot of his neighbors stood in the shade of a tree.

During the half hour or so we were there, the farmer poured out his gratitude to us, "the great señores from the north," as he called us more than once. He was, he insisted, a poor and miserable wretch, even though he had a farm large enough to graze thirty head of cattle. Without the assistance from abroad, he would be nothing, he said. He was profoundly honored that such important personages would deign to let their feet touch his humble piece of land, he said.

As disturbing as the performance was, none of my companions seemed embarrassed by it. When I wondered aloud, back on the road, if a fawning farmer was really what development was meant to produce, they looked at me blankly and talked about how well his herd was doing.

That farmer came to mind dozens of times last year as I crisscrossed Latin America and the Caribbean, researching this book on the Inter-American Foundation. Since 1971, the Foundation has been trying a different approach to development. Rather than fund projects designed by foreign governments, or by its own staff, it limits itself to direct support for those initiatives that come from the people the projects are supposed to serve. To visit some of the people the Foundation has supported in the last fifteen years, and to see the Foundation through their eyes, I traveled thousands of miles, from enormous, sophisticated, capital cities to tiny farmhouses, from slums to fishing villages, from Indian settlements in the tropical jungles to Indian communities high in the Andes.

I talked with Argentine government officials who, a few short years ago, were trying to stay alive under military dictatorship; with street kids who demonstrated the choke holds they once used to mug Bogotá pedestrians for their money, their watch, or the box of take-out fried chicken they were carrying home. I met a Peruvian social worker coordinating handicraft projects in Bolivia, a German anthropologist working with the Ayoréode Indians in the center of South America, an Italian priest in Quito, Ecuador, who runs a hostel for several

Development and Dignity

hundred Indian workers fresh from the sierra, a German biologist testing whether iguanas could be raised for food by Panamanian peasants.

I interviewed Jamaican lawyers who went into the Kingston slums and opened legal aid clinics, an Argentine bishop who defied death threats from his government when most of his countrymen were keeping quiet, Dominican Republic businessmen providing management and accounting skills to pushcart peddlers, Chilean kids from squatter settlements playing in a summer recreation program, Costa Rican farmers exporting their chayote crop to U.S. markets.

There were fishermen and priests, wandering puppeteers and rooted farmers, wood carvers and basket weavers, shop owners and small businesspeople, academic researchers and bee handlers, voluble storytellers and laconic Indians—all the jumbled mixtures and activities of the Western Hemisphere. And what they had in common, every one, was dignity. I became convinced that no matter how abysmal the economic level, how desperate the need for assistance, there is no point at which the dignity of the recipient is not more important than the aid itself.

The United States has been in the foreign assistance business since the 1950s. Most American taxpayers and most members of Congress have not been totally happy with the results. The American attitude is generally one part generosity ("we should help poor folks if we can"), one part skepticism ("the money probably doesn't get to the ones who really need it because their government officials squirrel it away in Swiss bank accounts"), and a dollop of resentment ("all we've given them, and they're not even grateful").

Gradually, I came to think that in the contrast between the farmer I had met years before in Paraguay, and the people I was meeting last year, lay important lessons about development and foreign assistance, about social and economic change, and about relations between people and nations. Many of those lessons are commonplace and fill the air whenever people who work in development gather: that there must be participation by the poor, that aid needs to reach the people at the base directly—it cannot be depended on to trickle down to them—that people need to help themselves, that the donor of assistance must be a true partner to the recipient. The air turns thick with the constant repetition of these lessons, but in project after project around the world they are repeatedly violated. No one questions them, but few know how to put them into practice. Indeed, many development agencies are prevented, by their very structure and the interests they serve, from carrying them out even if they wanted to.

In my attempt to distill the experiences of the Inter-American Foundation during the fifteen years since it opened its doors in March

Prologue

1971, I discovered that hundreds of knowledgeable people in Latin America and the Caribbean believe that the Foundation has found a way to assist and participate in the development process in their countries without distorting their goals or threatening their dignity. At a moment when U.S. policy towards the region is highly controversial, and often bitterly criticized, the Foundation, an official U.S. government agency, is widely regarded with trust.

As Americans gaze out, with growing consternation and bewilderment, at a Third World of countries and peoples we seem unable to understand, the fact that one U.S. agency has learned such lessons and put them into practice might light some candles on the road ahead as the world's richest country and many of its poorest move in uneasy harness, with both hope and foreboding, towards the twenty-first century.

PART ONE:
An Experiment

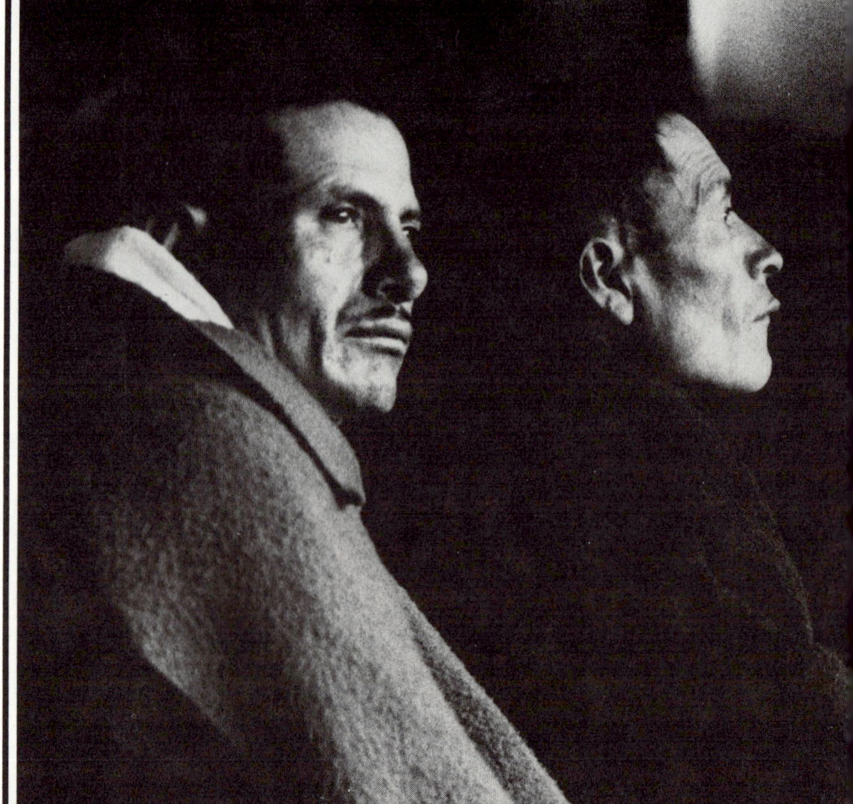

*The Foundation
Is Launched*

Chapter 1

Chapter 1

The Foundation Is Launched

THE INTER-AMERICAN FOUNDATION was born of reflection, not of reaction to a crisis. Foreign assistance programs created by the U.S. government, particularly those aimed at Latin America and the Caribbean, have typically emerged as a response to a perceived crisis. Thus, Fidel Castro's revolution in Cuba in 1959 was soon followed by the announcement of the Alliance for Progress. More recently, the Sandinistas' toppling of the Somoza family dynasty in Nicaragua, the threat of a guerrilla victory in El Salvador, and the appearance of a left-wing government on the island of Grenada spurred the announcement of the Caribbean Basin Initiative. That the U.S. government, like most human institutions, reacts to a crisis is not remarkable. We usually fix our roofs after they begin to leak. But a perceived political crisis may not be the best midwife for an economic assistance program.

The Alliance for Progress was an ambitious and much publicized effort aimed at alleviating poverty and underdevelopment in the Western Hemisphere. It was to be a partnership between the United States and the countries of Latin America and the Caribbean that would inject large amounts of capital and enlist the energies of people throughout the hemisphere to solve their problems. By the end of the decade, the physical signs of the Alliance were everywhere. On schools and buildings, on billboards at the side of new roads and highways, over the entrances to housing projects, irrigation projects, port facilities, and, in the most remote communities, on white sacks of grain, one could see the clasped hands that were the symbol of the Alliance. Despite all the signs, most observers agreed that the impact on poverty was marginal, that in fact the poor people of the region were more desperate, more mired in poverty, than they had been at the beginning of the decade.

Many in the United States could see the shortcomings of the Alliance. What was generally not understood was the bitterness with which many people in Latin America regarded it. "We had the experience of the Alliance," one dairy farmer in Uruguay said. 'We saw that it didn't reach the people who needed it, except for some bags of food, bags that had 'U.S.A.' written all over them."

A Colombian lawyer working with peasants recalled that, as a student, he and many others questioned the Alliance. "It came wrapped in an atmosphere of propaganda against Cuba. We could see it never got to the needy people. There were a lot of loans and you see the results today in the roads and bridges. But that hasn't changed mental attitudes nor the conditions of life of the campesinos."

A Colombian peasant said, "You always heard on the radio that so many millions of pesos or millions of dollars were coming. But you never saw anything. The local governments are a filter that's clogged. The aid goes in, but it never comes out on the bottom, or very little passes through."

To a priest in the Dominican Republic, the Alliance was "heavy handed." "There was an image of superiority," he said, "an irritating sense that they were big, powerful, and we were small, weak and poor."

The Right Idea at the Right Time

Dissatisfaction with the Alliance was rife in Congress as well. Hubert Humphrey in the Senate and a group of congressmen including Dante Fascell, Bradford Morse, John Culver, Donald Fraser, and Clement Zablocki, all members of the House Foreign Affairs Committee, were concerned that the programs of the U.S. Agency for International Development (AID) were too focused on abstract economic growth models and were not reaching the poor people for whom Congress intended them. During the late 1960s, they worked together on several pieces of legislation aimed at moving U.S. assistance closer to the poor.

In 1969, when Dante Fascell took over as chairman of the Subcommittee on Inter-American Affairs, he began a series of hearings on the Alliance, its goals, and its impact. "There was a general awareness in Congress," Fascell recalled, "that classical economic development, meaning the accumulation of capital, increased per capita income, infrastructure, and so on, had worked in Europe after the Second World War, but that in the Third World there was too much to be done. In many of those countries, 75 or 80 percent of the people were outside the social and economic mainstream of their countries. They weren't being reached by the assistance, and they weren't participating in any democratic way. We had this nagging concern that the social side of development was practically totally ignored and so we kept struggling to focus attention on that side of the problem."

"Over the next few months of hearings," said Marian Czarnecki, then staff director of the Foreign Affairs Committee, "we tried to pry out all the ideas and criticisms we could. We saw that after a decade of the Alliance, of spending a billion dollars a year, most of the money stayed in the States, or went to governments who were interested in building industries, and the average people saw very little sign of anything happening.

"So, out of those hearings came the feeling that the form as well as the direction of U.S. assistance had to change. We had to get away from political considerations. We had to have something steady, rather than a spigot that you would turn on and off with every change in policy or in relations between the United States and another government. We wanted to use some funds to energize people at the bottom levels of society to work for social change in their own countries, at the grassroots level."

After lengthy discussions, members of the subcommittee recommended creation of an independent agency, free to move in new directions. It should be able to support organizations of poor people directly, rather than going through their governments, which usually gave rhetorical approval to the idea of popular participation but in practice were unwilling or unable to implement it.

"Dante Fascell," Czarnecki said, "was the one man who drove the idea through." On November 6, 1969, the full House Committee on Foreign Affairs reported out a draft bill creating an Inter-American Social Development Institute. (Two years later, when the new agency was ready to begin operations, its name was changed to the Inter-American Foundation.)

The Committee report was specific about the shortcomings it saw in traditional U.S. foreign aid programs in Latin America:

> First, that during the past eight years all too little United States assistance has reached the masses of the Latin American people or made a visible impact on their daily lives;
>
> Second, that the social development goals of the Act of Bogotá, the Charter of Punta del Este, and the Declaration of American Presidents, whose objectives of expanding opportunity for the great majority of people form the very cornerstone of the Alliance for Progress, are not being achieved in any substantial, meaningful sense; and
>
> Third, that while Alliance for Progress programs operating at the government-to-government level had done an impressive job in promoting the industrial and economic growth of Latin America, they have proved much less effective in responding to the requirements of social and civic change on that continent.

The new agency would support "developmental activities designed to achieve conditions in the Western Hemisphere under which the dignity and the worth of each human person will be respected and under which all men will be afforded the opportunity to develop their potential, to seek through gainful and productive work the fulfillment of their aspirations for a better life, and to live in justice and peace." The legislation gave the agency a remarkable amount of leeway. It could work in practically any sort of development activity and with practically any individuals, groups, or organizations it chose, either in the United States or abroad.

The legislation stressed that the new institution should be independent from the rest of the government and, to that end, put it under a seven-member board of directors, four from the private sector, three from the government. With a fine congressional appreciation for the power that appropriations committees wield over federal agencies, it circumvented the usual governmental practice of one-year appropriations by providing the Foundation $50 million in funds that would be available until expended. On December 30, 1969, Congress passed the bill into law as part of the Foreign Assistance Act. Congressman Fascell, backed by Republican Bradford Morse in the House and Democrat Frank Church in the Senate, had mustered the necessary bipartisan support. The bill sailed through without floor debate in either the House or the Senate.

Finding Leadership

The Nixon Administration did not quite know what to make of the new agency it found when it returned to work after New Year's Day in 1970. It had not yet developed a foreign assistance policy, and was still awaiting the recommendations of the Peterson Commission, then making an overall study of existing policy and agencies. Despite misgivings within the Administration, the National Security Council recommended going ahead with implementation of the legislation, which principally meant selecting nominees for the Board of Directors. Viron Vaky and Arnold Nachmanoff, then Henry Kissinger's advisers on Latin America in the National Security Council, engaged in careful negotiations over the next several months to select nominees on the basis of their knowledge of Latin America rather than for reasons of political patronage, as the White House's personnel office would have preferred. Meanwhile, on May 25, 1970, President Nixon signed an order directing AID to transfer to the new agency the first installment of the $50 million provided for in the legislation.

On August 17, the White House announced the seven nominees to the board: Chairman—Augustin S. Hart, Jr., Executive Vice President of the Quaker Oats Company; Vice Chairman—George Cabot Lodge, lecturer at the Harvard Business School; Charles A. Meyer, Assistant Secretary of State for Inter-American Affairs; John Richardson, Jr., Assistant Secretary of State for Education and Cultural Affairs; Charles W. Robinson, President of the Marcona Corporation of San Francisco; Luis A. Ferré, Governor of Puerto Rico; and John A. Hannah, Administrator of AID.

When the announcement was made, Gus Hart was on a raft on the Salmon River with his wife and two youngest children. He had agreed to serve on the board, but did not discover until he came off the raft trip that he had been named chairman.

Development and Dignity

"Sometimes you never know why the White House calls you," Hart said, "but in this case I knew they were looking for people with some knowledge of Latin America, people who spoke the language, or enough of it so they could get along well. Our business took us down to the level of the mass market, and they said they knew our companies had shown a real interest in trying to help the little guy."

Quaker Oats had sent Hart to Latin America for the first time in 1946. "We had mainly an export business there and a couple of small plants. But as we got after it, things started to grow pretty quickly and we ended up with these manufacturing and marketing companies.

"At that time the big cry in business was if you wanted to be popular in these countries, you had to let local capital invest in your business. My experience led me to believe this was not a practical long-term strategy for being a good citizen of a country. I defended our 100 percent ownership, and said we shouldn't apologize for it. But I said we should be a good citizen by doubling or tripling the amount of our profits we normally gave away. And we should seek out worthwhile ways of giving it away. We got ourselves up to 5 percent of our profits, and we made our managers responsible for really paying attention to the things they gave the money for. We really wanted to help the little guy, not just give to the local American School."

Nachmanoff and Vaky had assembled a board experienced in Latin America and in the workings of the U.S. government. Like Hart, Charles Meyer had had a long business career in Latin America—with Sears Roebuck—before taking over the top State Department post for Inter-American affairs. George Lodge was a keen student of development in Latin America, and his book, *Engines of Change*, was influential in directing attention to the importance of popular participation. Charles Robinson's Marcona Corporation had created foundations in both Peru and Chile to provide economic assistance. Luis Ferré was, in Hart's words, "a bridge between the United States and Latin America." John Richardson, Jr., and John A. Hannah, like Meyer, came to the board meetings as individuals, contributing their experience, but they were also in a position to assist the Foundation as it took shape and to protect it in the inevitable turf struggles within the federal bureaucracy.

"The members of the first board," one long-time Foundation representative recalled, "were men of considerable stature. None of them was trying to make a name for himself here. They were men of accumulated experience in Latin America and with a very clear idea at least of what they *didn't* want this to be. Men secure in their own status, willing to take risks. They understood, and said, that much of what we tried was not going to work. That gave the staff

The Foundation Is Launched

a lot of freedom and produced a great deal of honesty. The grantees could be honest with the representatives, the representatives with the regional supervisor, and so on up the line. I remember the grantees were so honest it was hard to get them to say what was good about a project. They were so intent on telling you in detail what all the problems were.

"The early board members spent a lot of time at first trying to get the Latin American view of things. From what they heard, they concluded that the Foundation should not be an instrument of short-term foreign policy; that it should not take two or three years to decide on a project; and that it should be responsive. They all felt there was a lot of ferment in Latin America, a lot of people trying to do things, but that enthusiasm was dampened by delay and feasibility studies."

Fascell was impatient with the methodical approach of the board. "Dante got hold of me," Hart said, "and lectured me. It had been nine months since the legislation passed, he said, and we had to get going, show some action. But I wanted to study it first."

Hart hired consultants to review all the major sources of aid going to the region and to look for the gaps, for what still needed to be done. He stressed above all the mandate to be innovative, and gradually the board moved toward broad decisions about style of operation. It wanted the Foundation to reach the poor in Latin America and the Caribbean in ways not attempted by U.S. agencies before, and to do that it needed to know from the poor what *they* wanted to do and how they wanted to do it.

At the same time, Hart had management consultants search for candidates for the executive director of the new agency. "That produced a short list of four people. Meanwhile, we had several hundred letters about people who would be 'great' for the job, letters from people in the government, in the Congress, from all over. I had hired the consultant's firm for other reasons, but it turned out to be a great buffer. I just referred every recommendation to them, and no one ever objected to that process. In the end, we never hired anyone who came recommended from a political source."

Each board member interviewed the final four candidates. One of them was William M. Dyal, Jr., a former Baptist missionary who had spent nine years in Central America and Argentina, returned to the United States to take part in the civil rights movement in the early 1960s, and then joined the Peace Corps to run its program in Colombia and later its North Africa, Near East and South Asia region.

"Bill showed each of us a little more understanding of what we wanted to do than the other fellows did," Hart said. "Also, he had shown administrative ability with the Peace Corps. We all liked what he did in reorganizing the South Asia region."

"I guess they hired me because I was so off-the-wall," Dyal said. "I wasn't a traditional development expert." The board had come to believe there was no closed body of expertise on development in Latin America. They wanted this new agency to be open. "In my interview," Dyal pointed out, "I said the answers to development were there, in Latin America, not in the United States, and so we shouldn't have a rigid formula about how to operate."

Declarations of Independence

The board's choice of Dyal as executive director of the new institution raised hackles at the White House. "The head of personnel told me we would have to have our appointments approved by him," Hart recalled. "He said the President wanted it that way. 'The President told me exactly the opposite,' I said. 'Let's go ask him.' So he let it drop. But he asked if Bill was at least a Republican. I said I didn't even know. We got away with that and with a lot of other things as they came along."

Dyal had been assured that the Foundation would be completely independent, but doubts crept in as he sat down in Fascell's office for his first meeting with the powerful congressman from Florida's southern Dade County. "Fascell was smoking a pipe. No smile. He said that for months people had been coming to him with ideas for projects they wanted funded and he had been putting them off by telling them to wait until the Foundation was set up. He said that now he was going to send them all over to me, and he wanted to know if I was going to listen to them.

"I said to myself, 'Dyal, this is going to be the shortest job you've ever had.'

"'I'll listen to them,' I told him. 'If you send someone over, I'll definitely listen. But frankly, I doubt if we're going to fund any of them.'

"He just sat there and stared at me for a moment. Then he looked at some papers on his desk and said that he had some people in mind. He wanted to know if I would interview them if he sent them over for jobs. And I thought to myself, 'Here you go Dyal.'

"'I'll interview them,' I said, 'but unless they're the special kind of person I'm looking for, I have to tell you it's unlikely they'll get jobs.'

"And he just stared at me for a few more seconds, and then he suddenly slapped the desk. 'Goddamn,' he said, 'I think we've finally got what we need here,' and in my nine years at the Foundation, he never once made a demand on me. So right from the beginning, I knew we could act with integrity and that he would back us. It gave me a great deal of strength and confidence."

From his first day on the job, Dyal realized he would need backing. The Foundation was like a fish emerging from an egg. Its first task was to avoid being swallowed. Bigger fish were in the water. "There were $50 million in requests for funding on my desk when I arrived at the Foundation," Dyal said. Many U.S.-based, private, non-profit organizations with active programs in Latin America had been important supporters of the legislation creating the Foundation as it wended its way through Congress. They assumed that, once in operation, it would be the natural funder for their own projects. While the legislation setting up the Foundation did permit funding U.S.-based organizations, Dyal and the board, at a seminal meeting on May 5, 1971, decided that if the Foundation was to take a new and experimental approach, it must seek new avenues. Funding existing voluntary agencies would mean that the money would be spent in traditional ways. The Foundation opted for funding what Latin Americans and Caribbeans wanted, not what U.S. groups or individuals wanted to give them.

To the consternation of many U.S. groups, the Foundation announced that it would only consider projects drawn up and to be managed by organizations based in Latin America and the Caribbean. It further said that those projects should promote more equitable distribution of income, goods, and services and more participation in decision-making and should serve as models for replication. At one stroke, all the proposals sitting on Dyal's desk were ruled out. But, although the Foundation would not fund U.S. organizations, it left open the possibility of working through them under the right conditions. "We won't fund you, but we'll meet you in Latin America," was the way one Foundation representative summarized the decision.

Dyal and the board faced a host of other problems in putting flesh on the bones Congress had provided. Dyal returned again and again to the relationship he had with the board as a key to the freedom with which the Foundation took shape.

"I didn't mold the Foundation," Dyal said. "I was one part of it and was being molded myself. I was on a search. We all were, and we were willing to ask questions. We all had the same feeling about the need to be independent. I didn't want to be tied to short-term foreign policy considerations. The board didn't want to be just one more cog in the big government wheel. Gus Hart said, 'We're going to run this like a private business.'

"Those board meetings were some of the best learning experiences I've ever had. There was a camaraderie. The board members were there as individuals, not as representatives of government bureaucracies or other organizations. The idea was that they were bringing their own expertise. To emphasize that, we had a rule. If they couldn't attend a meeting themselves, they couldn't send a substitute."

Development and Dignity

A major challenge facing Dyal and the board was to establish the new Foundation's credibility in a region deeply suspicious of the United States—for good reason. "It was a time when suspicion about the C.I.A. was rampant," Dyal recalled. "I said it didn't matter what our rhetoric was. We would be judged on how we acted."

To allay suspicions, Dyal and the board decided that all the Foundation's files would be open. With the exception of personnel files, which were restricted by law, the Foundation would refuse to hold any confidential or secret documents. "I kept us out of all the cable traffic," Dyal said. "I was the only one at the Foundation with a top secret clearance. If anything came in that I needed to see, I had to go over to the State Department on the bus and read it there because I didn't want that stuff in the building."

Dyal could keep the Foundation away from the State Department, but could he keep the State Department and other agencies away from the Foundation? Especially in the early years, there was high-level support within the State Department for the Foundation's autonomy. Still, ambassadors are frequently insistent on their responsibility for anything the U.S. government is doing within the country to which they are accredited and, over the years, several have attempted to exercise veto power over Foundation funding. Increased discussions with embassy officials about the Foundation's program gradually helped head off such problems in most cases.

The decision to be outside the loop of U.S. foreign policy-making has demonstrated persuasively over the years that the Foundation is not part of the U.S. intelligence community. But if "institutional purity" laid the basis for trust in the region, it did not guarantee it.

"It took a while for the trust to build," Dyal said. "The Mexicans, for example, told us they had watched us for two years. 'We wanted to see how you worked in Central America,' they said. In Chile, Orlando Letelier, who was the ambassador in Washington then, said we were okay. Gradually, the early trust we built up spread like a grapevine in the region. But it was a personal relationship, hands-on, eye-to-eye. You have to build trust in something like this on the basis of a personal relationship. There's no other way. We all had to work at it. During those first couple of years, I often went to Latin America and the Caribbean to back up and reinforce what the representatives were saying about how we intended to operate. Those efforts and what we did in practice were what saved us from the climate of cynicism and distrust."

Perhaps the most crucial task Dyal faced was finding the right staff to implement the new approaches. One of the earliest decisions concerning staff was that they would not be permanently located abroad. The idea was to avoid building up another set of bureaucracies, however small, in other countries, and to minimize staff involvement

The Foundation Is Launched

in the projects being supported. It also would serve, Dyal believed, to keep the new Foundation independent of pressures from the local U.S. embassy.

In recruiting a staff, Dyal drew on his experiences in Latin America and in the American South where he had seen well-intentioned outsiders fail at attempts to bring change. "I saw imposed solutions that didn't take into account what the people wanted," he said. When he was interviewed by the board, Dyal said he was still very much on a search. "I knew I didn't want to bring a missionary approach to Latin America to the Foundation. I'd spent much of my life rejecting the missionary attitude that says 'we're going to teach you.'"

But Dyal had also learned some of the characteristics of effective development work. "My years in Colombia were a good learning time for me. I worked through a lot of my feelings about agents of change. But I could also see the advantages that Peace Corps volunteers and missionaries had in being close to the base. I could see that people who were good listeners were able to get things done. How people related, or didn't relate, was very important to me. So when I came to the Foundation, I knew I wanted listeners, people who were open and could identify with others. They needed to have good language skills and sensitivity to other cultures.

"But I wanted a balance between cultural sensitivity and tough-mindedness. I wanted people who were empathetic rather than sympathetic. I could have staffed the entire Foundation with ex-Peace Corps people, but I purposefully didn't. I wanted more of a mix. I was looking, not just for technicians, but for people who had a holistic view. I wanted people who could sit in the ambassador's office in the morning and talk to him and who then could get into a jeep or climb on a mule and in a few hours be in a campesino's house and be equally at home there."

Several of the early staff members did come from the Peace Corps, however. Another pool from which Dyal drew were former missionaries in Latin America. From their experiences on the ground, many people in both groups had become convinced that Latin American societies had to change fundamentally if they were to solve the overwhelming problems of poverty and social injustice. But Dyal stressed that North American activists were not the solution for the region. "When I came to work at the Foundation," one former missionary priest recalled, "Dyal said to me: 'You've been an activist and an advocate. This is a different job. You have to be an observer and an interpreter.'"

Dyal had learned, as had members of the board, that the region was full of people with initiative who were already at work on the problems facing their societies. All over Latin America and the Caribbean, people interested in the welfare of the poor had concluded that the much-advertised development aid was not trickling down or

Development and Dignity

would not trickle down in sufficient volume to make a difference. That conclusion reinforced an already widespread determination among thousands of people in Latin America and the Caribbean to take a piece of their destiny in their own hands. They didn't need outsiders to tell them what to do. All they needed, Dyal believed, were the resources to let them get on with it.

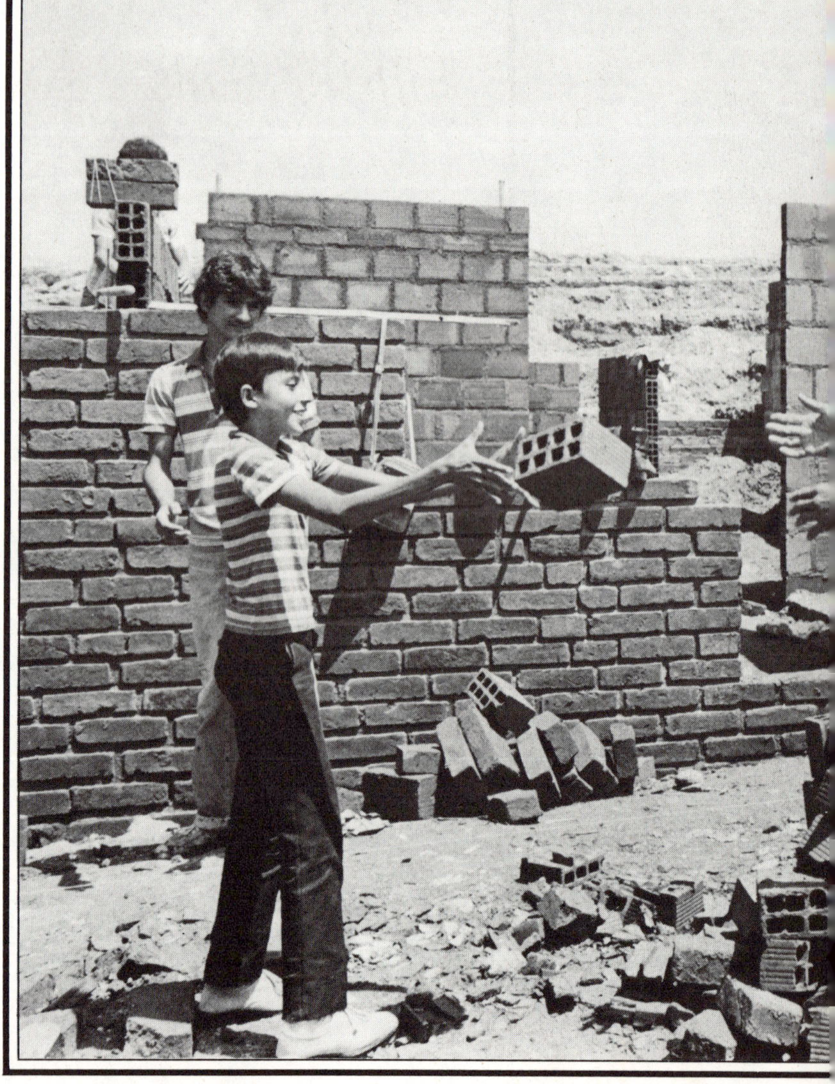

Southern Winds
Fill the Sails

Chapter 2

Chapter 2
Southern Winds Fill the Sails

IN 1966, HORACIO BERRETTA accepted a teaching position in the school of architecture of the Catholic University in Córdoba, Argentina. During previous studies in Europe, Berretta had been exposed to progressive Catholic ideas about social action, and imbued with the excitement of change in the Catholic Church growing out of Pope John XXIII's Vatican Council. He returned to his native Argentina with a sense of mission.

Córdoba is one of Argentina's major industrial cities, although it still preserves its colonial past in ancient churches and government buildings. It also boasts a national university renowned as the birthplace of an educational reform movement in 1918 that swept over much of Latin America. Visions of current reforms danced in Horacio Berretta's head when he joined the faculty at the Catholic University. But his colleagues proved more obdurate than he expected and rejected his proposals to link architectural studies to the resolution of one of Argentina's major social problems, the lack of low-cost housing.

However, a handful of students, among them Carlos Buthet, a first-generation Argentine of Swiss parentage, adopted Berretta's belief that architects should be at least as concerned with the housing needs of the poor as with the whims of the wealthy.

Attracted by its artistic dimensions, Buthet had decided on a career in architecture while still in high school. One vacation he joined a program organized by a local Catholic priest and lived in a poor neighborhood for a month, an experience, he said, that changed his life. "It raised all the fundamental questions: What am I here for, what is the meaning of life, and so on. It gave a direction to my interest in architecture."

Throughout Latin America other young people were undergoing similar experiences. Because the Catholic Church plays a central role in education in most Latin American countries, many students were influenced by the ferment within it at that time. Since the days of the Spanish conquest, the Church had been part of the power structure. Now it began to question its role. At first, its approach was paternalistic, directed toward palliative attempts to satisfy basic needs rather than fundamental changes. But as it began to implement the social encyclicals of the nineteenth and twentieth centuries which taught that there was a social responsibility inherent in being a Catholic, young people all over the continent began to respond.

Having experienced Argentine poverty directly, Buthet welcomed Berretta's ideas about new roles for architects. Blocked from creating a new program within the faculty, Berretta, joined by Buthet and a handful of other students, opened a center for the study of low-cost housing. They began to investigate housing conditions in the makeshift shantytowns called *villas de miseria* around Córdoba.

In the 1950s, an industrial boom had changed the face of the old colonial university city. Argentina's automobile industry was centered in Córdoba and a myriad of smaller supply industries grew up around the manufacturing plants. The new jobs drew thousands of people from rural areas and continued to do so up until the mid-1970s. Those who found steady factory jobs moved into Argentina's lower middle class, while others survived more precariously on the fringes of the boom economy and in the villas.

Berretta and the students began to assist residents of the villas who were interested in working together to rehabilitate their homes. Later, they designed low-cost housing that could be built collectively by the future owners. They invented new techniques and materials for low-cost construction, several of which they since have patented. Gradually, their primary goal shifted from housing structures to the social solidarity that could be encouraged by people working together to meet their needs for housing and services such as water and electricity. The organization they founded, now known as AVE (Asociación para la Vivienda Económica—Economical Housing Association), includes about thirty professionals—architects, sociologists, social workers, and an economist. The guiding philosophy continues to be based on progressive Catholicism and the belief that man best fulfills his nature and destiny as a member of a community.

The winds of change sweeping over Latin America blew not only from Rome and from cities such as Medellín, Colombia, where the Catholic bishops gathered to discuss the role of the church in unjust societies. Fidel Castro's revolution in Cuba generated a political hurricane in the Caribbean, and its winds buffetted the most remote corners of the continent. Students in Latin America were particularly attracted by the idea that change was possible, that Latin America was not necessarily doomed to suffer forever under an exploitative social structure.

"I was of the generation that left the classroom to go to the countryside," Fabio Londoño said late one night at a streetside restaurant in Cali, Colombia. In the 1960s, Londoño quit the university and started teaching literacy in a poor urban barrio, and later worked for five years with peasant organizations. Then he returned to finish his legal studies. "We resumed our careers, but not the traditional careers. We wanted to continue working for social change."

Cali sits in the Valle del Cauca, Colombia's richest agricultural valley. Huge sugar cane plantations cover much of the valley floor.

Cattle graze in the rolling foothills, and peasants raise food crops in the mountains. Many of the peasants also hire out as day laborers, providing the seasonal labor force to cut cane and transport it to the smoking sugar mills. Hundreds of thousands of peasants left the countryside, driven by poverty and widespread violence which broke out in the late 1940s. But social tensions, fueled by the intense concentration of land ownership in a few hands, continue to characterize rural areas. Peasants with land often find themselves caught in legal snares by more powerful neighbors and stand in danger of losing crucial water rights and even their small holdings. Landless peasants have turned to *tomas de tierra*, the occupation of fallow land on the huge estates, in desperate attempts to secure a livelihood.

Londoño and some colleagues began to provide legal services to peasants and eventually developed a mobile law office mounted in a jeep. Three days a week they visit rural communities in the southern half of Valle, developing cases and offering courses on legal matters affecting peasants.

"We see the law as an element of social change," Londoño said. Like the architects in Córdoba, for whom housing construction is less important than the changes in people's attitudes toward themselves and their society, Londoño sees lawsuits as means rather than ends. "We don't want passive clients," he said. "We don't want them to leave a case totally to us. We insist that they participate in the process. They must attend to some of the details themselves so that they get familiar with the legal process. For example, there was a problem in one community where one family had control of 80 percent of the water. We found provisions in the law that permitted the others to pipe water across that family's land. But the final steps were taken, not by us, but by the local community leader. We prepared him with the legal arguments, but he did it. And he won the case."

An Innovative Style

The Inter-American Foundation's directors and new president didn't know about Horacio Berretta and Fabio Londoño when they began to chart a course for their new agency. But they knew that all over the region, people like Berretta and Londoño were applying their talents to the problems of their societies. In deciding that the Foundation would try to support such people, they were consciously turning their backs on the approach traditionally taken by official development assistance agencies. The assistance bestowed by these agencies has been criticized often, and bitterly, over the past quarter-century. Because of the failure of assistance to trickle down, some critics have called it a system for taxing the poor people of rich countries for the benefit of the rich people in poor countries. But an even more

Southern Winds Fill the Sails

fundamental criticism is that, too often, development has been what specialists in rich countries "do" to people in poor countries. Problems are defined, programs planned, and projects designed *for* the supposed beneficiaries rather than *by* them. Participation is routinely cited as a necessary ingredient in the success of a development project, but too often it has meant only free or cheap local labor to implement a project drawn up far away.

In traditional U.S. development assistance, the diagnosis of the problem, the prescription, and the initiative to put it into effect came from the United States. The early leaders of the Inter-American Foundation were more modest in approach. "We knew from our own experience that we didn't have all the answers," Gus Hart said. But they also knew from their experience that people like Berretta and Londoño were finding their own answers. "Latin Americans had proven competence in a variety of fields," said Charles Meyer, another original member of the board. "I'd known that for years. Gus Hart and I shared this attitude from our experience beating the Latin American bushes for Quaker Oats and Sears Roebuck." Bill Dyal had come to the same conclusion from his missionary and Peace Corps experiences in Latin America.

In deciding to restrict the Foundation's role to responding to Latin American and Caribbean initiatives, to backing activities like those Berretta and Londoño had already begun, Dyal and the board had set the Foundation apart from most other development agencies. The Foundation would not be an initiator of projects, an agent of change. It would act more like a venture capitalist on the lookout for good ideas to bet on. It would not have master plans that laid out funding priorities for each country. Above all, it would be innovative.

Despite the determination to be innovative, the Foundation staff found it difficult at first to break out of the traditional channels of development funding. Their assumptions about social and economic development were conventional. They sought out projects intended to meet a basic need in a traditional sector such as housing, employment, access to credit, or rural development. Their initial contacts tended to be with local organizations already plugged into the international funding networks. By the end of 1971, the Foundation had approved four projects, all from organizations that had previously received international assistance.

But if its first steps were in familiar ruts, the Foundation was at least innovative in its style. It began work with no specific institutional criteria by which to choose among projects. Early choices were determined more by the perceptions and judgments of individual staff members than by a shared conceptual framework. But some criteria quickly emerged—the Foundation was very cautious about imposing solutions from the outside, one of the reasons for its decision to fund Latin American and Caribbean groups rather than U.S. organizations. It preferred to support action rather than research. And it favored relatively short-term projects to avoid making the grantees dependent on the Foundation.

Gradually, the Foundation staff began to see that some of the national development organizations with which they had first worked often took a paternalistic stance. They were trying to do for the poor what they thought the poor could not do for themselves. This inspired the staff to seek out smaller groups working at the local level and usually not reached by international funders. As time went on, the Foundation would focus more and more on local communities striving to improve their lives with their own ways, means, and time frames.

Meanwhile, the Foundation's understanding of development and social change deepened through experience. Initially Foundation staff believed that projects designed to meet a basic need in an identifiable sector, such as housing or job skills, would lead to social change, but they gradually grew more aware of the complexity and interrelatedness of social problems. This more mature perspective was discussed in an early internal document: basic needs and sectoral problems were seen as but "manifestations of a complex social process inextricably related to human needs, values, and political, economic, and social systems. Greater attention was given to multidimensional programs such as integrated rural development, strengthening of popular organizations, promotion of local culture, consciousness raising, worker self-managed enterprises."

The Foundation's thinking about criteria for funding projects had also deepened and broadened. Gradually, new considerations came into play when a proposed project was examined:

- Were the intended beneficiaries involved in both design and implementation of the project, and were they aware of its consequences?
- If there was an intermediary group between the Foundation and the intended beneficiaries, was it accountable and open to them?
- Would the project empower a group to solve problems it thinks important and to better understand the world it lives in?
- Was there potential for the benefits of a project to spread beyond the group originally involved?

Of course, few projects satisfied all the criteria, but the direction in which the Foundation was moving was set. The effectiveness of projects was no longer judged solely by measurable standard-of-living terms, but by more qualitative gains, such as "greater esteem and sense of identity, greater access to the tangible and intangible offerings of the society at large, greater voice, increased leverage to achieve objectives, recognition individually among peers and institutionally in the greater society," to quote again from an early internal document.

Gradually, as the Foundation extended its contacts in the region and discovered the variety of local initiatives underway, the projects it funded began to look like a mosaic of life in Latin America and the Caribbean. Soon, the Foundation was involved in what the people of Latin America and the Caribbean were most busy doing: building houses, telling each other stories, producing art, growing food, fishing and farming, raising bees and dairy cows and iguanas, weaving clothes, moving to the cities, finding playgrounds for their children, getting pushed around and cheated, and defending themselves.

By accepting as the starting point what the people of the region were doing and wanted to do, the Foundation also gave up the rigid categorization of projects that is typical of traditional development assistance. And this, too, fit in with the approach taken by Dyal and the early board members. "We refused to get into category funding," Dyal said. "I learned from an old campesino leader in Bolivia that you can't categorize projects. 'We don't think about health on Monday, crops on Tuesday, child care on Wednesday,' he told me. What we wanted to do was touch the grantees wherever they happened to be, knowing that this touching could only be part of a much greater process."

As a result, Foundation-supported projects are often hard to categorize, and, when they are forced into categories, their more ambitious aspects disappear. Housing projects, like the one in Córdoba, for example, are really aimed more at contributing to the experience of organization and joint effort than to erecting physical structures. Projects that improve the ability of artisans to get decent prices for their products often are after much more than the generation of income. They are concerned with the preservation of quality, with artisan traditions, and eventually with matters of human dignity and identity.

These goals were not always present in the projects. Often they emerged as initiators of projects grew in their understanding of what they were engaged in. In the beginning, many project initiators were professionals simply expecting to apply their technical skills to the solution of problems among people more unfortunate than themselves. With time and experience, they gained a deeper understanding of the human dimensions of their activities and grew firmer in their conviction that the human being must stand at the very center of the development process, as the subject and not the object of that process. By choosing to back them, the Foundation was also choosing to accompany them on a voyage of discovery of themselves and their societies.

PART TWO:
Preservation and Change

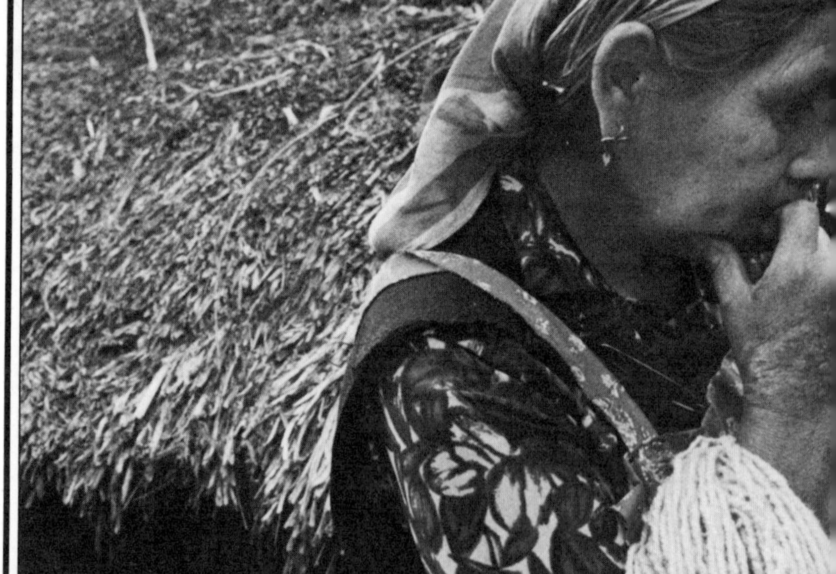

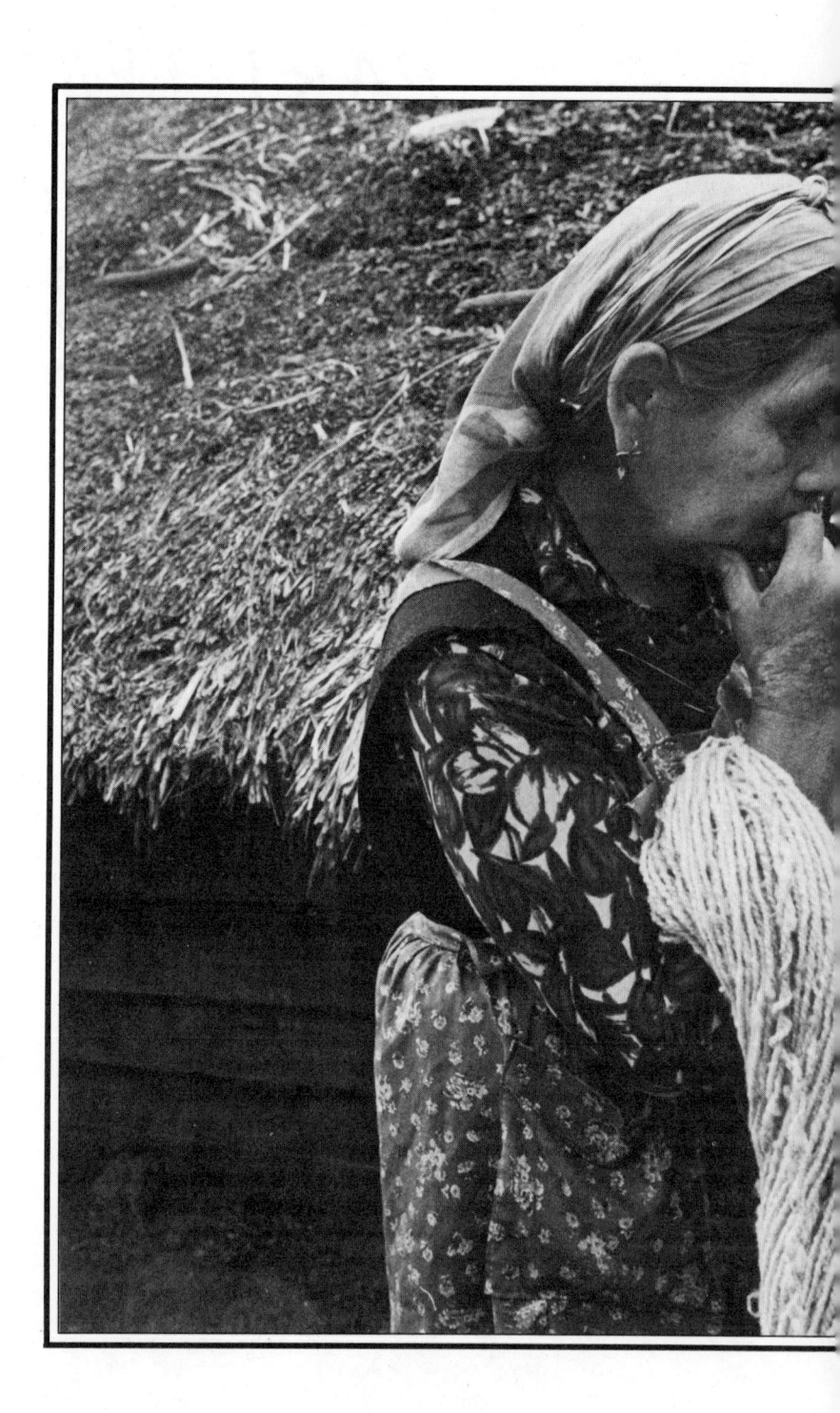

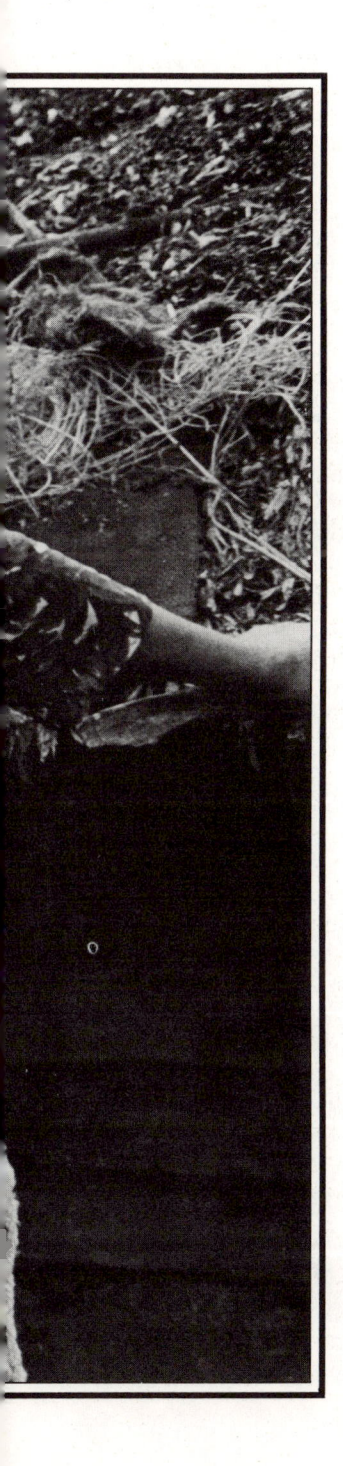

*A Sense
of Identity*

Chapter 3

Chapter 3
A Sense of Identity

"WHO AM I? Where do I come from? Where do I fit in?" In the gloom of a late afternoon in Quito, while storm clouds rumbled overhead, Juan García recited the questions that have driven him to become a one-man folklore commission for his people, the descendents of black slaves first brought to Ecuador in colonial times. Shelved on the office wall behind him were hundreds of tape cassettes filled with interviews, five years of his work. During those five years, the Inter-American Foundation has supported García as he searches the river banks of Esmeraldas in Ecuador's coastal lowlands or the dry hillsides of the Chota Valley for the old men and women who carry in their heads the history, legends, stories, and poetry of their race.

Juan García's questions are asked frequently in Latin America and the Caribbean. They are voiced in Spanish, English, Portuguese, French, Creole, or in any one of dozens of Indian languages, sometimes in tones of intellectual curiosity, sometimes in pain and anger, often in desperation. The questions touch on some of the most serious and sensitive problems in the region: the tension between ethnic identity and national integration, the destructive effects of racial prejudice, the struggle for cultural independence and personal identity and dignity. The efforts to find answers to those questions have taken many paths, some of them violent. In several cases in recent years they have involved the Inter-American Foundation in unique projects and carried it toward a more complex understanding of development.

Development is usually thought to mean change for the better in material standards of living, or at least to be aimed at that goal. If the material standards of living are to be improved, many other kinds of changes in a society are usually required. Most development agencies, therefore, are in the business of social change. *They Know How*, a book about the Foundation's first five years, summarized the sorts of projects the Foundation supported and identified "changes in relationships" as the common denominator. Most of the people who came to the Foundation for backing were working for changes in the patterns of use, ownership, and distribution of land; in forms of ownership, management, and employment in the workplace; in access to and control of credit, capital, and commodity flows; in the observance of human and civil rights; and in the treatment of minorities.

A Sense of Identity

But a small number of Foundation-backed projects indicate there is another element to development besides change: sometimes people must first fortify their base before they sally forth to change the world. No matter how poor their material conditions, people always have resources: intelligence, imagination, language, the skill of their hands, history, a sense of identity, a cultural heritage, pride, a certain piece of land. Sometimes the development process is not so much about change as about the preservation and strengthening of those resources. Without them, Juan García's questions go unanswered.

García's questions go back to his school days. His father was a Spaniard who arrived on the Esmeraldas coast of Ecuador around 1940, dedicated himself to mining, and married a local black woman. "Down on the coast, we have a saying, that one takes in his culture with his mother's milk. If your mother is white, you're white. If she's black, you're black." But in school, he began to wonder where he fit in. "The identity of Ecuador is Spanish and also Indian. The Indians have managed to insert elements of their traditions into the schools. There are monuments to Indian leaders. But as a black boy in school, I had the problem of not finding anything in Ecuador to identify with. School children learn of Indian and Spanish heroes. But nothing of the blacks. No one identifies with the blacks, and blacks find no ancestor mentioned in the history books they read in school. There are no monuments to blacks."

García was born near the sea, and his earliest memories are of swift trips to market in southern Colombia, riding the Pacific currents in outrigger canoes. Then came the long return, poling the canoes through the dim light of the mangrove swamps and spending the nights in isolated houses on stilts above the river bank while old men spun stories. As a young man, he continued to travel and eventually wound up in Bogotá, the Colombian capital, where he ran a small factory. He frequented the university, took some classes, and talked with students. "There I learned that one ought to have a cultural tradition. I began to think about Ecuador. I decided to return to my own country to do something. I didn't know what."

Back home, he found himself caring for his dying grandfather and teaching in the local school. His grandfather's illness was prolonged. "It's because he knows so many secrets," the people said. "He can't die until he passes them on." The grandfather started to tell his stories and legends to García. "That's what began my interest in the old people and the hoard of stories they have. And then I began to look in books. Who are we, the blacks in Ecuador? Where did we come from? And there was nothing. No one knew anything. No one had written anything.

"I began to travel the rivers in my own canoe to talk with the people. Whenever I'd see an old person, I'd stop to talk. And I began

29

to see that there was a marvelous treasure in all the traditions but that it was going to die out. I started to think: Why not try to gather this material? But I didn't have the means to do it right. I talked to a woman who could make *guarapillo*, a medicinal drink, and she told me she picked one hundred herbs to make it. How was I to remember the names of a hundred herbs?

"I went to a foundation here in Quito and they suggested I write a proposal, and they would send it to someone." García didn't know anything about the Inter-American Foundation, but one day someone introduced him to Chuck Kleymeyer, the Foundation's representative for Ecuador. "I told him what pained me most was the loss of this tradition, because every time I went back on the rivers, another old person had died," García recalled. Kleymeyer accepted García's invitation to see what he meant. They traveled together by road to the mouth of the Santiago River, and then in a dugout canoe with an outboard motor for one hundred kilometers up and down the river and its tributaries.

"The Foundation came through," García said. "I could get the equipment I needed to record. And I just went out and started taping. *Décimas* at first, our poetry. And then other things started coming out, legends that even I hadn't heard before. There were stories of white and black magic, of a man who could turn into a hen or a bunch of bananas when the police came into his house looking for him. The police would kick the hen out of the way or take two bananas, and afterwards, the man would limp or be missing two fingers."

Some of the stories told of dark bargains that people would strike with the devil so they could become wealthy. In one, a man raises a family from a dozen eggs he hatches with incantations, and his sons and daughters become, as he intended, expert thieves, rustlers, pirates, spies, who amass great wealth for him. In another, a godfather violates the baptism ceremony by willing the priest's blessing to bypass the infant and enter a coin he holds in his clenched fist. The infant is left spiritually adrift, but the coin now has the magic power to attract all other coins it comes in contact with and to bring them home to its master. Such stories of conjuring up dark powers bespoke the powerlessness of the slaves' lives.

Other stories recounted the history of Ecuador's blacks, how their ancestors were brought down from Colombia, how some gained their freedom by fighting in the war of independence, how emancipation finally came in 1860, but only after the slaveowners were recompensed. There were religious stories, children's stories, tales of animals very like the Br'er Rabbit stories from the American South.

As García probed deeper into his people's folklore, he began to see in the old storytellers the monuments he had sought in vain as a schoolboy. "I realized they are the only monuments we have. But no one is going to make a monument of them. So I said to myself, the next best thing to a monument is paper. Get it down on paper.

"Now, the question is what do we do with this material. I want to give it to the young people. I want to be sure that other black children don't have the problem I did of lacking a sense of identity. See how alienating the educational system is? Nowhere, not in stone, not on paper, do you find our people remembered. And this is a serious problem for the integration of the nation. It tells you you're not here, you don't exist. That's what this work is aimed at."

Of some seven hundred hours of interviews already taped, García has transcribed over one hundred. He has published nine booklets containing samples of the collected material. He hopes that it can be gradually introduced into the educational system. But he knows that his real work is for posterity. "This collection probably won't be used for years, until the country realizes what it has lost. Especially the black people. In fifty years, maybe, someone will come looking for it, saying, 'There was a guy named García who collected stories.' That's why I'm working."

Meanwhile, he has rekindled interest in the old storytellers. "In some places, we were able to reactivate the tradition of storytelling by the old people. What happened was we would visit the house of a storyteller and arrange to go back the next day to record some stories. These houses have large open areas. We would bring a few packs of cigarettes. And gradually, other people would come by, old people, youths. Sometimes we'd be there until dawn. Afterwards, the youths would ask us where we were going the next day. And so, during a month we'd spend in a small town, we'd revive a whole tradition."

An Outpost of English

A dozen years ago, about the same time that Juan García returned to Esmeraldas, a young North American teacher on an extended trip wandered into Cahuita, a town south of Limón on Costa Rica's Caribbean coast. Paula Palmer says she was just looking for a good beach when she came to Cahuita, but what she found was an opportunity to help preserve a unique culture that was starting to disappear, a task that has consumed her ever since. "I guess I was something of a hippie," Palmer said. "I'd worked in the civil rights movement at home and then traveled through Mexico, where I worked with some Indian groups, and then kept moving until I got to Costa Rica."

Discovering that Palmer was an experienced teacher, a woman in Cahuita urged her to prolong her stay and to teach her seven grandchildren English. Palmer didn't understand why the woman was so insistent, but she agreed. When she appeared for the first class, thirty-five children were waiting. Palmer called a parents' meeting and discovered the interest in English instruction for their children was intense. Soon she had eighty-five students and no reading materials.

Meanwhile, Palmer had been learning the Creole language common in the Limón region, as well as the local history. The English-speaking black population of the region originally came from the Caribbean islands. Some were fishermen and hunters who had followed the droves of turtles up along the Panamanian coast. Later, farmers from Jamaica came to settle. Still later, jobs on the banana plantations and the railroads drew many more.

Until mid-century, the Limón region maintained its distinctive cultural identity. People went to English schools; links were maintained with Afro-Caribbean people from other parts of the Caribbean basin. A rich theatrical tradition flourished. "They were doing *Macbeth* in Puerto Viejo in 1915," Palmer said.

Changes came in the 1950s. President José Figueres was intent on integrating the nation and breaking down the barriers that separated Limón from the rest of the country. Under Figueres's policies, Spanish took over from English in Limón's schools. As it did, Palmer said, "the people began to lose everything the English schools had done, all the cultural activities, which had formed a sense of being Afro-Caribbean."

As she listened to the older people recount the history of their community, it occurred to her that she could use their stories for her English classes. She began recording the oral history and then transcribed it. As the stories circulated in the community, neighbors urged her to collect full time. They were aware that many of the old people were dying and with them, links to their own past. After teaching three years, Palmer followed their suggestion. Two more years of recording led to her book, *What Happen: A Folk History of Costa Rica's Talamanca Coast.*

"But even though the adults were very interested," Palmer said, "they were concerned that their children were not. That led me to think I should be teaching the high school kids to collect their history themselves, rather than having me do it. And that's what we did."

A local agricultural cooperative, many of whose members were parents of Palmer's students, presented a proposal for research on the local culture to the Inter-American Foundation and made Palmer coordinator. Soon many of the local youths were busy gathering material. "People have told me that it was important that I was a foreigner," she said. "They said the kids took it from me that this history and these traditions are rich and fascinating. They wouldn't have listened to their grandparents saying the same thing."

The gathering of oral history led to the renewal of cultural events and practices that had faded away. For the first time in twenty years, the people began to observe Slavery Day, a celebration commemorating their liberation. A cricket match was played for the first time in thirty-five years. Special ceremonies honored the old people of the community.

Eventually, the students gathered enough material for three publications on the history, culture, and economy of the black and Indian populations of the region. Impressed by their quality, the Costa Rican government reprinted them in Spanish for distribution throughout the school system to increase public awareness of the country's heritage. But Palmer believes the project's main impact will be felt among the people of the coast. "More important than what we can teach the rest of the country about this region is what goes on in the souls of these thousand or so kids and what they'll do in Costa Rica because of the way they feel about themselves."

Flutes and Drums

Children, and how they feel about themselves, are the focus of another Foundation-supported project aimed at preserving cultural resources—this one in the remote and beautiful city of Sucre, Bolivia. Sixty percent of Bolivia's six million people are Indian and the rest are *criollo*. The line is drawn more by culture and history than race. An Indian is a person who comes from an Indian community, wears Indian dress, and speaks one of the Indian languages. A criollo is a white or *mestizo*—usually an urban person—who speaks Spanish.

Since the conquest, "Indian" has also meant the people who have been exploited. Avid for the mineral wealth of the Andes, the Spaniards herded Indians into silver mines and then onto the haciendas that grew up around the mining centers. Institutionalized systems of mandatory labor preserved the serf-like condition of the Indian for more than a century after independence. A common practice called *pongiaje*, from the Aymara word for door, required that an Indian had to protect the landowner's house every night by sleeping curled up in the doorway. Even today, the word *indio* is so weighted with connotations of oppression and degradation that it is considered an insult. The more neutral term, *campesino*, has replaced it in polite language.

Despite advances since the 1952 revolution, chasms of distrust separate Indians from criollos. Many Bolivians insist that the political instability and economic chaos for which their country is famous are only surface manifestations of these deeper rifts. They see scant possibility for genuine national development until there is both self- and mutual respect among the peoples of Bolivia.

But when a group of youngsters plays the haunting music of the Andes, Bolivia's discordant culture suddenly seems a bit closer to harmony. Cultural harmony is represented in the instruments: the guitar brought from Spain; the *charango,* an Indian version of the guitar, its body fashioned from an armadillo shell; and the fur-trimmed drums, the *quenas* (flutes) and *zampoñas* (pan pipes) that are as Andean as the snow on Illimani's peak. Together, they produce a rhythmic, piercing music tinged with the desolation of the altiplano.

Several years ago, a group of university students in Sucre formed a group called Los Masis to play Andean music. Their practice sessions in local parks sometimes aroused the ire of passersby. Sucre is perhaps the best preserved colonial city in all of South America, and it had always preened its Spanish heritage, which included a deprecatory attitude towards all things native. Until 1952, no Indian wearing traditional garments dared even enter the city's central plaza.

However, when word filtered back from Paris and Rome that groups playing Andean music were the rage, many Bolivians began to listen with greater interest. During the 1970s, Los Masis prospered. They released several records and traveled thousands of miles on concert tours. But as its members finished their university studies and moved on to other careers, Los Masis broke up. Those who chose to stay with music began to teach local children and eventually opened a cultural center.

Since 1980, the center has offered nightly classes in guitar and Andean musical instruments. In its workshop, students are taught to make as well as play the traditional instruments. More important, they learn to value their own culture, a culture which for centuries has been scorned, leaving the people born into it with Juan García existential questions. "A child will come in here crying," said a teacher in one of Sucre's poor barrios, "because someone called him an Indian. They have lovely legends, lovely traditions, but they're not valued, and so they don't value themselves. The problem is how to learn to value those things again, in the face of a modern world that devours tradition."

For Jorge Arduz, president of the Los Masis cultural center, solving that problem is an indispensable part of development. "The most important factor in any kind of development," he said, "is the human factor. To be productive, man has to value himself, which means being able to understand where he stands in society and in history. That's why for us cultural development goes hand in hand with economic development."

Culture Is a Place

The projects described above are all based on the faith that if a fading cultural patrimony can be restored, it will strengthen the capacity of people to deal with the challenges that surround them.

A Sense of Identity

But can it be demonstrated that such faith is justified? If people can answer Juan García's questions confidently, will they be more successful at solving other problems? Perhaps the best place to ponder that question is from an island in the Gulf of San Blas, on Panama's Caribbean coast.

When a Kuna Indian awakens on one of the small coral islands where most of his people live, his gaze wanders past the thatched houses of his neighbors, out over the low-riding canoes of farmers headed for their mainland plots, and then across a mile or so of shimmering water to a mass of green forest rising, virgin and luxuriant, to the ridge of the San Blas mountains. At his back, the sun climbs above the calm Caribbean, and its first rays loosen the tufts of mist snagged like fleece in the clefts of the hills. For generations, this dawn panorama, serene and unchanging, has greeted the Kuna people.

But if that Indian were standing atop the 2,400-foot-high San Blas range, the view down the other slope would be less reassuring. Large swaths of thick vegetation have fallen victim to the machete and the torch. Ash-gray tree trunks stand above the denuded landscape, skeletal remnants of the once-towering jungle.

For several years now, peasants from the increasingly arid interior of Panama have been slashing and burning—implacable as soldier ants—towards Kuna land. Cattle ranches, producing beef for the international market, drove many of them from their farms, and cattle are close behind them again. In three or four years, when the newly cleared and shocked land will no longer support subsistence crops of bananas, rice, corn, and manioc, they will plant pasture and try to sell their holdings to the ranchers. In a few more years, the fragile soils will be so leached that even cattle-ranching will fail. The tracks of the future can be read on the southern slopes and lower ridges of the San Blas, where the erosion that will inevitably claim all the cleared acres has already begun.

Until recently, Kuna lands seemed safe from this depredation. Although less than a hundred miles from Panama City, they were practically inaccessible until the government announced plans to push a branch road from the Pan American highway over the ridge and down the northern slopes of the San Blas to the Caribbean coast. The Kunas were of two minds about the road. They welcomed the prospect of easier movement for themselves and their goods between San Blas and Panama. But they knew that the road had already brought settlers to the southern slopes, and they feared encroachment on their own land. With a fine sense of geopolitics, they realized that the point of maximum danger was a place called Udirbi, where the new road would enter their territory. It was there that they had to establish a presence.

First they attempted to carve out their own agricultural colony in the virgin forest. When that failed because of the poor soil, the Kunas began to explore the idea of creating a park for scientific research. As the plan developed, they saw major advantages in such a park. Twenty square kilometers around Udirbi would have clear, patrolled boundaries to bar intruders. Moreover, if the threat persisted, the international scientific community, handed an expanse of unstudied rain forest rich with unique flora and fauna, would be an influential ally in future struggles.

Eventually, the Kunas presented a proposal to the Inter-American Foundation. With Foundation backing, and support from several scientific and conservation agencies, as well as AID, they are now building housing and research facilities at Udirbi and cutting nature trails to observation sites in the forest.

The completion of the park should forestall a serious threat to the land of the Kunas, but their determination to protect it springs from impulses much deeper than considerations of property rights. To the Kuna, this land is not just a physical resource, but a spiritual one as well. "We say that this land is our mother," Leonidas Valdez explained. Valdez is one of the three *caciques*, or chiefs, who are the principal spokesmen for the entire Kuna people. Kuna traditions say the green-clothed earth is the body of the Great Mother. In the beginning, they say, she was naked. Her union with the Great Father produced all of the vegetation—which became her garments, the animals, and finally humans. "The land is also the culture," Valdez continued. "Here are born all things necessary to our culture: the fronds we use for the puberty ceremonies, all the foods gathered for our communal feasts, the materials our artisans use, and what goes into the construction of our houses. All of it comes from the forest. If we were to lose this land, there would be no culture, no soul."

The Kunas have no trouble answering Juan García's questions. They are one of the very few Indian peoples to have survived into the twentieth century with their culture, their society, and their identity intact. Because of their self-confidence, they have been able to approach Western culture like careful department store shoppers rather than awe-struck primitives. They pick through the wares of Western culture, select those ideas and techniques that seem useful, and then tailor them to their own traditions. All this, the Kunas believe firmly, is because they have their base in the land to which they return for replenishment and reinforcement. Their experience suggests that self-confident people, who know where they come from and derive personal security and group pride from that knowledge, are best prepared to accept and implement the changes their societies need.

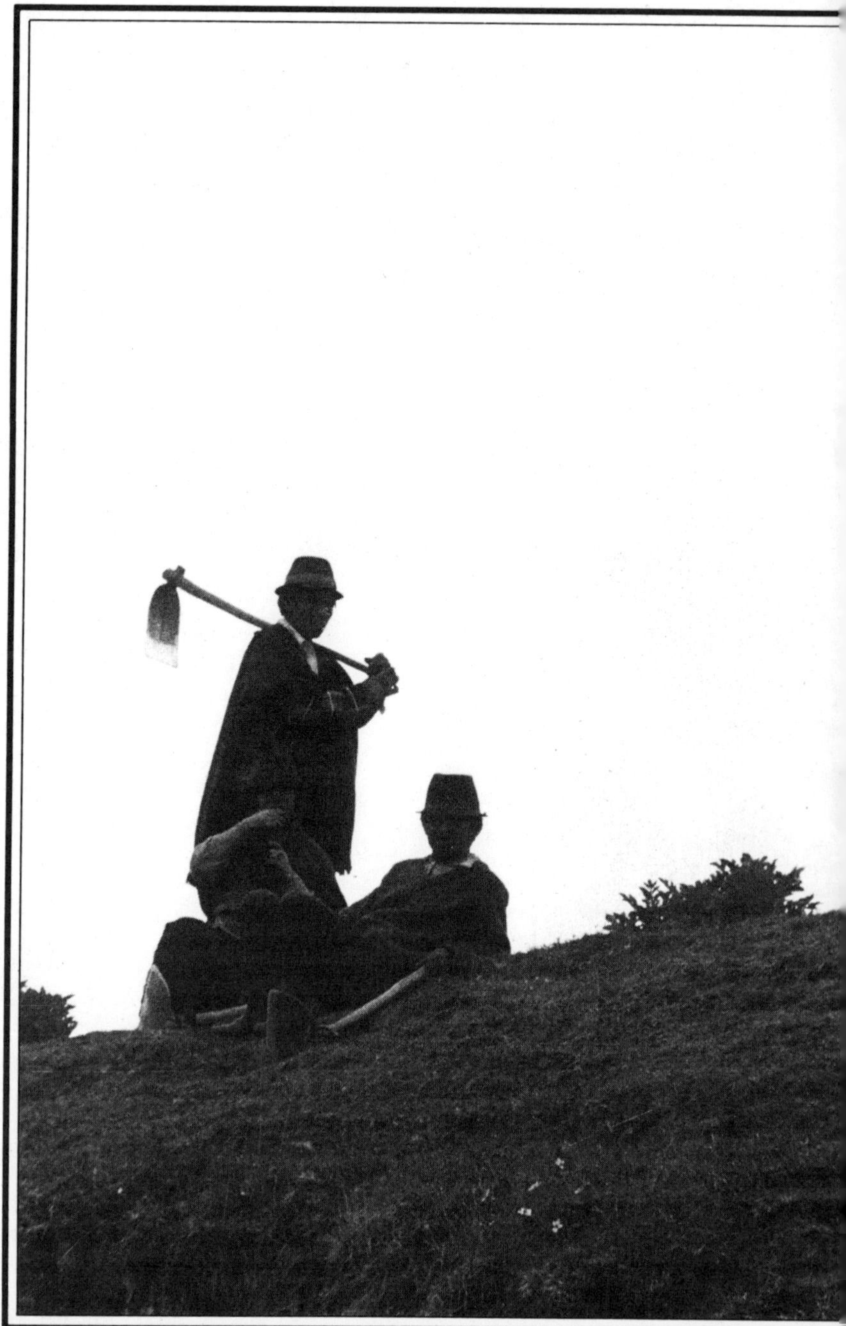

The Troubled Countryside

Chapter 4

Chapter 4

The Troubled Countryside

IT IS HARD to get a farmer anywhere to say things are getting better, but the dairymen who belong to the Sociedad de Fomento Rural (Rural Improvement Society) in Durazno, Uruguay, sometimes come close.

One chilly August night, Pablo Bomfrisco, his wife, and their two young daughters sat in their small farmhouse. The glow from the city of Durazno, just under two kilometers beyond a low ridge, lit up the stormy sky. Mrs. Bomfrisco was asked about the changes in their lives after the society began processing milk on the outskirts of Durazno two and a half years ago. "It's marvelous since the plant opened," she said. "He's here now instead of running around like a crazy man delivering milk."

Before the plant opened, with the help of an Inter-American Foundation grant, milk producers near Durazno rose early for the morning milking, then loaded their raw milk onto small wooden carts, hitched up the horse, and drove into the city. From 7 to 11 o'clock every morning they would make their rounds, delivering milk to their clients, frequently passing one another in the streets as they crisscrossed the city. Often their customers would claim they didn't have the right change. "The milkman was always the last to be paid," Pablo Bomfrisco recalled.

Farmers who couldn't go into Durazno would sell their milk to a middleman, at his price. That system worked all right in the fall and winter when production dropped, but in the spring, when it rose, the middleman might not buy milk every day if he had enough of his own.

Bomfrisco still rises early to milk his cows, but now he takes the cans only a few hundred yards down to the main road at the entrance to his farm. Soon, a neighboring dairy farmer will be by in the society's truck to pick up the numbered cans and deliver them to the processing plant.

Last August, the plant was processing 17,000 liters of milk a day. A labeled sample is taken from each can and evaluated for quality, cleanliness, and cream content. Producers are paid according to their milk's quality, and milk that doesn't meet the standards is rejected.

The quality test, besides safeguarding the plant's reputation, is the basis for the extension service the society provides its members. An agronomist advises the producers how to increase production, improve

The Troubled Countryside

hygienic conditions in the milking sheds, and control their herds for disease.

The plant pasteurizes the milk and bags part of it for sale in Durazno and nearby communities. The rest is turned into butter, cheese, and yogurt and stored in the refrigerated rooms on the bottom floor for later sale.

Now that Bomfrisco sells his milk to the plant, he is free from the milkman's grueling rounds. He no longer has to live the day-to-day existence of a peddler, badgering his customers for a few pesos—which he must turn right around and spend on some already postponed need of his family. Now he has a stable income, winter and summer, based on the number of liters he produces. His family can budget their expenses and see what they have every month. "We're in control now," he said.

He has time to take his children to school, to work on his farm, or to consult with the agronomist or veterinarian at the society's office. If he needs credit from a bank, his production record at the plant is proof he can handle the loan.

The plant has rationalized distribution, put the farmers in control of their daily rounds, provided more time for families, and insured a stable income. "What that really means," said Wilfredo Gelos, president of the society, "is that the plant has given dignity to the dairy farmer."

The Sociedad de Fomento Rural in Durazno is one of Uruguay's most successful cooperatives. It has 1,411 members, over 90 percent of the farmers in the region, including a former president of the country. While exiled in Uruguay, Brazilian political leader Leonel Brizola was also a member. "If he becomes president, we'll sell lots of cheese to Brazil," Gelos joked.

About four hundred of the members are dairy farmers. The others produce grains, wool, meat, and vegetables. Many of the services the society provides them began with the help of an earlier Inter-American Foundation grant. The society store sells seeds and farm supplies. There are facilities for drying and milling grains and for repairing and renting farm machinery, as well as technical assistance services.

The story of the society in Durazno is not all idyllic, however. There have been crises and failures. Production plans for garlic, onions, and tobacco collapsed during the 1970s. Cheap food imports hurt local producers. In August 1985, with 140,000 kilos of cheese cooling at the plant, dairymen worried about competition in the international market from cheap Italian cheese. Still, the society has succeeded in bringing dignity, stability, and hope for a better future to the countryside around Durazno. Perhaps the best indication of its success is that young people there are staying on the farms. To visit Durazno is to see what the majority of the rural people of Latin America and the Caribbean aspire to, but usually fall short of.

A Harsh Reality

Visitors to Latin American cities who see more than the modern hotels, central plazas, government buildings, and comfortable residential areas are often shocked at the desperate poverty in the slums that ring so many of them. When one realizes that most of the people in those slums came from the countryside, and that most of them have *improved* their lives to some degree by the move, one begins to sense the true dimensions of rural poverty.

The mass of rural people are desperately poor. Despite decades of talk and some action, land reform in much of the region is more a rallying cry than a reality. Most of the peasants who have a small plot of land can barely support a family on it and are usually in debt to a local *patrón*. Millions supplement their meager income or the subsistence crops they grow with seasonal work as agricultural laborers. Families are divided for months at a time, as women stay at home to tend the fields while men go off to work on large plantations, often in distant parts of the country, sometimes across national borders. Millions more lack land entirely and survive by some form of rental or sharecropping arrangement and seasonal labor.

The ameliorating effect of government services, particularly in health and education, are often lacking in rural areas. It is the promise of such services that draws many rural people to the urban slums.

But perhaps the most tragic aspect of rural reality is that in many places things are getting worse. In fact many of the master plans designed to solve national economic problems are accelerating the crisis for the rural poor. As export-oriented large-scale agriculture expands throughout the region, in part in hopes of paying the crushing foreign debts many countries have incurred, the already-precarious position of the peasants worsens. They are forced from their land at the same time that rural jobs are disappearing in the face of increasing mechanization.

The rural crisis is not a new phenomenon. Peasants are often seen as mired in rigid patterns, unwilling to chance a new technology, but the truth is that their resistance to change comes from centuries of enduring wrenching, often devastating changes. Many of those changes were the result of colonialism, political or economic or both, that brought countries, or parts of countries, into the international economic system. Colonial policies often brought changes that threatened people, cultures, and land and other natural resources. Throughout much of the Andes, Indian populations are still suffering the consequences of the upheaval wrought by the Spanish conquest almost half a millennium ago. In the nineteenth century, when the newly-independent nations of the region became suppliers of food crops, minerals, and other raw materials to the international market, rural

The Troubled Countryside

areas were changed in ways still being felt today. The roots of today's warfare in El Salvador, for example, reach back more than a century to the spread of coffee plantations that undermined a communal land system and created a mass of landless peasants.

Since 1972, the Inter-American Foundation has put much of its efforts, and the largest chunk of its money—almost $90 million out of a total of just under $212 million—into the rural areas of the hemisphere. In several years, funding for agricultural and rural development has taken close to half the total funds spent. Between 1972 and 1985, 42 percent of Foundation grants have gone to rural areas. In all, the Foundation has made close to a thousand grants in the Latin American and Caribbean countryside. The vast majority of them seek to help people who have organized to improve their economic prospects. Sometimes the help required is a small sum to solve a particular local problem. Sometimes it is support for consumer or production cooperatives. Sometimes it involves backing ambitious campaigns aimed at the social transformation of an entire region. This wide range of Foundation projects reflects the variety of problems which afflict rural Latin America and the Caribbean today.

The Nicoya Peninsula

Until the 1930s, Costa Rica's Nicoya Peninsula was inhabited mainly by Choluteca Indian peasants and some settlers who had drifted in from Nicaragua. Much of Costa Rica's population was concentrated on the *meseta central*, the volcanic valleys around the capital, San José. As that population swelled, new settlers began moving down towards Nicoya, bringing with them cattle and coffee bushes. By the 1960s, they far outnumbered the Indians and controlled most of the best lands on the peninsula. The original inhabitants of the zone retreated to its fringes. There was a boom in beef exports during the 1960s. Highways were opened into the region. The settlers cleared even more land for pasture, which soon brought on erosion, and borrowed to finance larger cattle herds. When beef prices dropped, many began to sell out, and land concentration intensified.

Well-financed development initiatives have been introduced to solve the problems of low incomes, deforestation, rudimentary technology, and lack of marketing systems. Along with other funders, the Inter-American Foundation is supporting one of the most dynamic of those initiatives, the Centro Agrícola Cantonal (Agricultural Center) in the canton of Hojancha. Each of Costa Rica's eighty cantons has an agricultural center, a sort of steering committee made up of local farmers and representatives of government agencies working in the area. In Hojancha, the center has helped introduce a steady market for dairy production, a sophisticated reforestation program, a huge coffee processing plant, bee hives, better seeds, cheaper fertilizer, and a demonstration farm crammed with succulent crops, hygienic pig pens, and ideas about appropriate technology.

"We can already see the impact of these projects in the fact that the population here has stabilized. People have stopped leaving," one official at Hojancha said. But few of those projects seem to involve many of the older inhabitants of the canton, the "non-entrepreneurial, colored people *(gente de color)*" as he described them.

Teodoro Pérez is a dark-skinned, sinewy fisherman from Puerto Thiel who belongs to the agricultural center in the neighboring canton of Nandayure. Puerto Thiel, a hamlet of some thirty houses on the southern shore of the Gulf of Nicoya, is one of the fringe areas where the descendents of Nicoya's original inhabitants can be found. It is surrounded by large farms and ranches where many of its people, without land of their own, hire on. "I've worked since the age of seven as a peon," Pérez said. "But I've always been interested in progress. Not to get rich, but you have to leave something for the next generation."

Pérez believes strongly in organization as a way for poor people to progress. Starting about ten years ago, he helped organize his neighbors in Puerto Thiel to get electric lines strung into the hamlet and later to get pure water piped in. He urged the other fishermen in Puerto Thiel to form a cooperative and, when he met a representative from the Inter-American Foundation at the agricultural center in Nandayure, he promptly invited him out to Puerto Thiel to hear about their plans.

"Once a peon, always a peon," Pérez said. "It's hard to get away from that. We've got no land. It costs too much to rent land, plus all the rest of the investment in seeds, insecticides, preparing the land, and so on. And the banks won't give us loans. So we work as peons for the landowners. We know they've been exploiting us for a long time and that we're being replaced by technology, by machinery. We turned to fishing, but even there we're still working for the landowners. The cattle ranchers own the boats, even though they don't fish themselves. They just invest in boats and hire peons, and we wind up with 25 percent of the catch."

Still, Pérez and a score of his neighbors reasoned that fishing was their only hope. "We know the gulf," Pérez said. "And we know how to fish. We are experienced, professional fishermen. Also, we know that you don't fail with fishing. It's reliable." They formed a cooperative, figured out what equipment a fishing business would need in Puerto Thiel, and then sought help from the Inter-American Foundation. Based on past experience with other fishing ventures, the Foundation staff suggested some modifications in the plans for a building and equipment to store the catch and then approved funds for a small ice factory, nets, ten outboard motors, and ten large dugout canoes. The canoes were delivered at the end of 1985. "This is what the community needs," Pérez said. "A business will help everyone. As I told my companions, you've got to look ahead. Be ready for crises. If we don't have a business installed here, it's going to be much worse for a workingman. He won't be able to help his family in the future."

Learning the Market

Cooperatives are popular in Costa Rica. Many of them started in the 1960s, when the country's land reform legislation began to transform thousands of agricultural laborers on large estates into small landholders. Up on the *meseta central*, the typical rural community boasts a cooperative store where members buy farm tools, clothing, seeds, and fertilizer and where they can pay their electric bills. In theory, the government's extension service should reach the small farmer, but many farmers complain it does so only sporadically. Many of the cooperatives, therefore, have hired their own agronomist. Some, like the one at Tierra Blanca de Cartago, have already moved into processing and selling their members' produce.

Tierra Blanca was organized as a savings and loan cooperative in 1966, as farmers in the area struggled to recover from the effects of the 1963 eruption of Irazú Volcano, whose slopes they till. Since they resumed planting, around 1968, their cooperative has grown steadily. In 1973, it became an agricultural services cooperative, and the list of services it provides has grown apace: credit, farm machinery rental, a supermarket, a housing program, a medical clinic staffed with a doctor, and, with a grant from the Inter-American Foundation, a processing plant and warehouse for the figs, potatoes, carrots, and onions that thrive in the volcanic soil. Before, up to one quarter of the production was lost because of size, deformity, or minor damage. Now, much of that can be processed. The plant's production is sold in Costa Rican supermarkets under the cooperative's brand and exported to Guatemala and Panama.

Another agricultural export enterprise got underway in 1983 in the nearby Ujarras Valley where forty-seven farmers growing *chayotes*, a pale-green squash, formed a cooperative. There is a market in U.S. supermarkets for chayotes, especially in neighborhoods with Latin populations, but, until the cooperative was formed, exports and profits were in the hands of middlemen. A grant from the Inter-American Foundation helped the cooperative greatly expand its volume, from 600 boxes a month to 9,600.

To see whether other cooperatives in Costa Rica could profitably enter the export market, the Foundation recently backed a pilot project by local businessmen to offer them marketing assistance. ADIAME, the Asociación de Instrucción y Ayuda en Mercadeo y Exportación (Association for Training and Assistance in Local and Export Marketing), is a non-profit organization designed to put Costa Rican cooperatives and small producers in contact with national and international markets.

Jaime Cabezas, a San José businessman who is president of ADIAME, said a basic problem is that "many producers don't even know the final destination of their products, nor what qualities affect the price. They don't know the market. We will put prospective buyers in touch with the producers. Also, most of the small producers here don't know about the technical assistance agencies that could help them. We've studied the field to identify those agencies and found that the available technical advice is greatly underused. So we can be a contact there as well. This is all still very experimental, but if it works here, the Foundation could try it in other countries."

The Dispossessed

Sociologists contemplating the countryside draw a distinction between farmers and peasants. Simply stated, the term farmer is applied to those who work the land as a business, think in terms of profit and loss, are open to innovation, and adapt their practices according to a rational calculation of market conditions. Peasants, in this analysis, hold to the land for reasons more complex than simple economic ones, think more of survival and subsistence than of profits, and only grudgingly give up traditional methods. Any dichotomy applied to people tends to exaggerate differences, but the distinction does emphasize the different types of obstacles to rural development. The projects described above benefit people who would be on the "farmer" side of the dichotomy, who frequently lack only a certain resource (a credit fund, an organization, technical advice) to improve their ability to compete in the marketplace. But millions of rural people in Latin America and the Caribbean suffer more intractable problems. For them to compete requires changes—in mental attitudes, in social relations, often in the distribution of power. Over the years, the Foundation has backed numerous projects grappling with the need for such changes.

Down toward the tapering end of the South American continent, in the foothills on both sides of the Andes, live the remnants of the proud tribes of the Mapuche Indians. The Spanish conquistadors, whose march to the south was finally stopped by the Mapuches, celebrated their bravery in a great epic poem. Not until late in the nineteenth century, about the time the United States was subjugating the west, did the Mapuches finally succumb to the armies of Chile and Argentina. Ever since, most of their descendents have lived in abject poverty.

Bishop Jaime Francisco de Nevares estimated that in Argentina's Neuquén Province about 12,000 tribal Mapuches live in isolated communities scattered throughout the cordillera. "They are the poorest of the poor," he said. "They have the poorest land. That's their main problem. On much of it, a goat is the only animal that can survive."

The Mapuches sell wool, goat hair, and hides to earn the money they need for food. Until recently, their only commerce was with *bolicheros*, non-Indian store owners, who bought their goods cheaply, sold them food dearly, and charged exorbitant interest rates. In 1977, Bishop de Nevares began to encourage the formation of consumer cooperatives in the cordillera to break that exploitive economic system. A network of five cooperatives, the Cooperativas Indígenas de Neuquén, was set up. It has since grown to eleven serving over four hundred families. The diocese contributed three vehicles, including one truck, to link the far-flung communities, to supply their stores, and, as the cooperatives moved into marketing, to carry their goods to a centralized warehouse erected on diocesan land. In 1982, the Inter-American Foundation joined the diocese in supporting the cooperatives and is currently funding efforts to add six more to their number, to provide a radio communications link among them, and to increase training for cooperative members to overcome problems in management and in animal husbandry that a Foundation-funded evaluation pointed up last year.

Across the Andes in Chile, another church-based project is helping Mapuche communities solve basic problems of subsistence. The Obra Rural Metodista (Methodist Rural Work) has been active for forty years in the provinces of Cautin and Malleco, building schools and health centers on Mapuche reservations and starting an agricultural training center and extension service. In 1982, Obra Metodista decided to support a plan to improve the subsistence levels of 850 Mapuche families by encouraging production of vegetables and other food crops. Soon afterwards, the Foundation agreed to back the project. Leaders from the Mapuche communities were trained to grow the crops and provided with money for a revolving loan fund to make seeds and fertilizers available to peasants participating in the program. The project offers training in preserving food, in family and child nutrition, and in hygiene to community groups requesting it.

Success in such projects is measured in small increments. The Mapuches occupy the bottom rungs on the economic ladders of their respective countries. The immediate challenge facing them is survival, both as individuals and as a people. Marginal improvements in income and a slightly greater variety of food for the table can be the difference between more-or-less normal development for a child and a stunted body and clouded mind. Marginal improvements can help the Mapuches survive on their land, keep their families and their communities together, and perhaps encourage their attempts to organize themselves for protection against the exploitation and injustices their societies regularly inflict upon them. Throughout the hemisphere, many minority groups face similar challenges to their survival. In the poorest countries, the majority of the population must face them.

Tet Ansanm (Heads Together)

"There are a thousand places in Haiti where you could find a little water to save and a bit of ground to irrigate with it and people would live better," Bernard Etheart said. As a young man, Etheart went to Germany on a scholarship to study pharmacy. His contact with students from all over the Third World influenced him to switch to rural sociology. He returned to Haiti and started a center, the Institut de Consultation d'Evaluation et de Formation du Personnel, to help groups of peasants plan community development activities. He has seen relatively small projects transform many rural communities, but even he was doubtful anything would help Chambrum, a tiny community a few miles northeast of Port-au-Prince on the arid Plaine du Cul-de-Sac. "My solution for Chambrum," he said, "was two buses. Pack the people up and put them somewhere else."

The reason for Etheart's initial pessimism becomes clear on the approach to Chambrum. A rutted dirt road leaves the highway and follows a canal carrying irrigation runoff from the Haitian American Sugar Company plantations. The surrounding vegetation is all brush, scrub, and cactus. After a mile or so, the road veers from the canal and loses itself in trackless flats as smooth, hard, and devoid of life as the tarmac at the international airport a few miles to the west. If Haiti had stock car races, this would be the place to run them. On the far rim of the flats, the tiny, thatched, wattle and packed dirt houses of Chambrum come into view. About 800 people live in Chambrum, sustained by the goats and sheep they raise on the arid land.

"Obviously, the problem here is water," Etheart said. "One day, Marcel Duret, a friend of mine who runs a chicken farm nearby, came to me and said we should do something for Chambrum. That's when I told him to get two buses. But he insisted. So we started thinking about water. It's complicated and expensive. There's a layer of brackish water not too far underground. You'd have to drill through that to a second layer of sweet water. You'd need a pump. The Foundation paid to have an engineer do a feasibility study. He came out, looked everything over, and realized there was no need to drill or to pump. Just take water from the runoff canal, he said. It turns out that the community used to get water there, but several years ago the sugar company dredged the canal and lowered the level. All that was needed was a simple dam to bring water up to the level at which it would flow into the fields."

AID had already provided Chambrum with assistance to improve its roads and to build a bridge and a school. The Inter-American Foundation, in addition to supporting the engineer's study, had provided funds for leadership training, education, and the formation of community groups. The Canadian International Development Agency (CIDA) granted the money for construction of the dam. Etheart got an *animateur*, a community development worker from the town of Croix Fer, where a large-scale irrigation project was underway, to work with the people of Chambrum. They organized themselves in work gangs to divert the canal, so the dam could be built, and to dig the network of irrigation ditches through Chambrum's bone-dry fields. The project took four months.

The runoff water that once emptied into the sea now is directed by a V-shaped concrete dam into a thirty-foot-long concrete channel and then into five-foot-wide dirt ditches. Simple metal gates control the flow. Stretching away from the ditches are row after row of sweet potato plants, corn, sugar cane, and sorghum. A training program is introducing new crops, such as tomatoes, which can be marketed in Port-au-Prince. A bit of simple technology, a few tons of concrete, and four months of digging have made Chambrum's fields blossom.

The dam at Chambrum is a classic development project. The human need was great. The problem was obvious. The solution, once a technician was called in, was simple. All that was lacking was some outside support, since the community couldn't afford to build the dam on its own. The results are impressive. The people have more food for their own consumption and the possibility of cash crops for income. A community has been helped to survive in a harsh environment. All this, only a short car ride from the capital and the international airport, makes Chambrum a convenient showcase for foreigners visiting the projects of any of the several institutions which contributed to it, including the Inter-American Foundation.

But given the needs of the rural people of Haiti, it is clearly only a drop in the sea. Etheart himself volunteered the information that not all his Haitian colleagues were enamoured of the Chambrum project. "Marc Noel criticized it," he said. "He thought it happened too fast, that there wasn't enough organization of the people. I know what he means, but my argument was that without water there was nothing to keep the people here."

Marc Noel is a Haitian agronomist who grew up in Port-au-Prince. He got the incentive to work in the countryside from the Catholic priests under whom he studied. He spent several frustrating years

Development and Dignity

("thirteen years of failures," he said) working with various foreign development agencies. With support from the Inter-American Foundation, he now directs a project aimed at organizing rural people in the area around Gros Morne in northwest Haiti. "Over the last fifty years of misery, Haitians have lost much of their sense of community," Noel said. "That's one of the real sources of our underdevelopment. But we believe the sense of community is not completely lost, and so we try to encourage nuclei, and to duplicate them. I'm convinced that any development project must start with organization. Organization is first. Not motivation, not infrastructure. They come later, and are built on organization. Organization means awareness. And you must make the people aware of many things at the same time. Not only the need for change, but the reality of what can be done, and at what risk. For this country, now, I think it's the only way."

In addition to Noel's project, several Foundation-backed efforts in Haiti have concentrated on increasing awareness and organization among the poor people of the countryside. One of them is around Pilate, in the mountains between Gonaïves and Cap-Haïtien. "What interested the Foundation in this project," said Father Pollux Byas, a Haitian priest, "was that while its aim looks economic, it is really educational. There have been cooperatives and credit unions all over this country, and they die because the members lack education. If you want to develop the area, first you must put the heads together, *tet ansanm* as we say in Creole. You must have the sense of community, and you must have awareness. The eyes of the people must be open. They must have a vision of the world, their own world. If they understand that, they can infer for themselves to the broader world. They understand Duvalier by understanding the local authorities." (Two months after this conversation, Jean-Claude Duvalier fled a rising tide of popular protests, ending a family dictatorship that had controlled Haiti for almost three decades.)

Chimborazo

The belief is widely held in the hemisphere that only through expanding organization can the people at the bottom make progress toward guaranteeing their survival and then move on to fuller participation in their societies. Wherever possible, the Inter-American Foundation has supported attempts to widen the impact of development programs beyond the individual community to the surrounding region. In the countryside around Chimborazo Volcano, near Riobamba in the Ecuadorian highlands, the Foundation has backed an education campaign serving some two hundred scattered Indian communities.

Through the years, Chimborazo has been the setting for various development efforts. Most of them were designed by outsiders and

The Troubled Countryside

have made little significant change in either rural poverty or the sense of stigma with which the Indians have lived. The Foundation made an exception to its general policy of supporting private rather than government initiatives in 1979 when it decided to support the popular education program. Because this program had developed from the perspective of the Indians themselves and was built on a respect for their language and culture as well as an interest in their educational and economic needs, the Foundation believed it was worthy of support.

The program, run by an autonomous division of the provincial Office of Education, is based on teaching literacy in both Quechua and Spanish. Its aim is to help Indian peasants emerge from the prison of poverty and prejudice to which the conquest condemned them four and a half centuries ago. Thus it combines elements of social change and of the preservation of native values discussed in the previous chapter.

When Ecuador's legislators approved a nationwide effort to raise literacy levels, they left it to local authorities to implement the program according to the characteristics of each province. In Chimborazo, the provincial minister of education placed Carlos Moreno in charge and told him to hire his own team.

"I was a physical education professor years ago, when I first started working," Moreno said, "but I always had had an interest in social action." By 1968, he had become director of education for Chimborazo province. Later, he directed a volunteer program under an AID contract and then worked in non-formal education. He studied in the department of education at the University of Massachusetts before returning to Chimborazo to head the new literacy program. "What has always motivated me to this kind of work in this region," he said, "is having been born in an Indian community and having lived through all the problems that brings."

Ecuador's legislature had given the program specific goals: reduce illiteracy, contribute to economic and social development, and encourage the poor to organize and to participate in national life. Moreno set up the Chimborazo Department of Permanent Popular Education and recruited an eighteen-member team. In addition to literacy classes, they hoped to offer training of teachers and community leaders, a bilingual newspaper, promotion of small rural crafts and industries, and cultural activities aimed both at restoring respect for the Indian culture and at encouraging reflection in the communities about the issues that affect them.

"The Foundation grant enabled the team to put these ideas into practice," Moreno said. "The government's program only included money for salaries for teachers. The Foundation gave us what we needed for an integrated program, not just teaching people to read. Above all, the Foundation respected what we were trying to do."

Development and Dignity

A central part of the program, made possible by the Foundation's grant, is the Feria Educativa, a group of musicians and actors drawn from the region who visit the communities regularly, performing Andean music and putting on puppet shows and improvisations based on the particular problems affecting each community. Feria Educativa works both to reinvigorate the Indian culture and to use it to help people solve their problems. "We were being taught that our culture was worthless," one of the young members of Feria Educativa explained. "Radio was replacing our traditional music even at our celebrations. People were selling their musical instruments to anthropologists. But with our work, people have begun to see that our music is worth something, and many younger people have formed musical groups. Now there are more than fifty groups like Feria."

Some of the physical changes the program has brought to the region can be seen in the community of Cebollar Alto. Its one thousand people live among heavily cultivated, slanting fields at an altitude of 3,800 meters. The low, heavily-thatched roofs of their adobe houses blend into the landscape like haystacks. The community center is a group of buildings on a flat knoll overlooking a narrow valley and surrounded by the high mountains. Next to a volleyball court are several buildings with tin roofs housing the organizations and activities that have sprung up in Cebollar Alto in the past five years: a bakery, a textile workshop, a library, and a meeting place for the community. The bakery was the first communal activity. People from Cebollar Alto once had to go to the market in Riobamba where, they said, the merchants sold them stale bread at high prices. Now their own bakery produces fresh bread three times a week. The profits are spent on supplies for students in the literacy program, maintenance of the bread oven, and financing other community projects. Meanwhile, the members of the committee responsible for the bakery learn the bakery trade as well as bookkeeping and other skills needed to run a small business.

As the program has spread through the mountains, Moreno said, the amount of resources contributed to each community has gone down because the people are contributing more. "Putting up the communal house used to cost a hundred thousand sucres," he said. "Now it costs closer to twenty thousand because the community puts in more. In many cases, we put in only the door and windows, which cost about twelve thousand, and this means we can reach even more communities with the same amount of money."

But more important than the buildings, bakeries, and workshops, Moreno said, are the changes in attitudes. "When we started, there was opposition in the communities to literacy teaching in Quechua. People wanted to deny they were Indians and to speak only Spanish. Now their pride in being Indian has increased, and that changes they way they look at the outside world." But such changes in attitudes are not universally welcomed. When gasoline prices rose a few years ago, thousands of Indians gathered in Riobamba to protest, provoking the governor to complain to Quito that the program was stirring up trouble. "But President Osvaldo Hurtado backed me up. He said that Indians being able to think and act for themselves was what the literacy campaign was all about. Another time, a minister complained to me that an Indian he'd met was rude. He said he wasn't humble enough. That wasn't the right word. These are humble people, but they are no longer humiliated people."

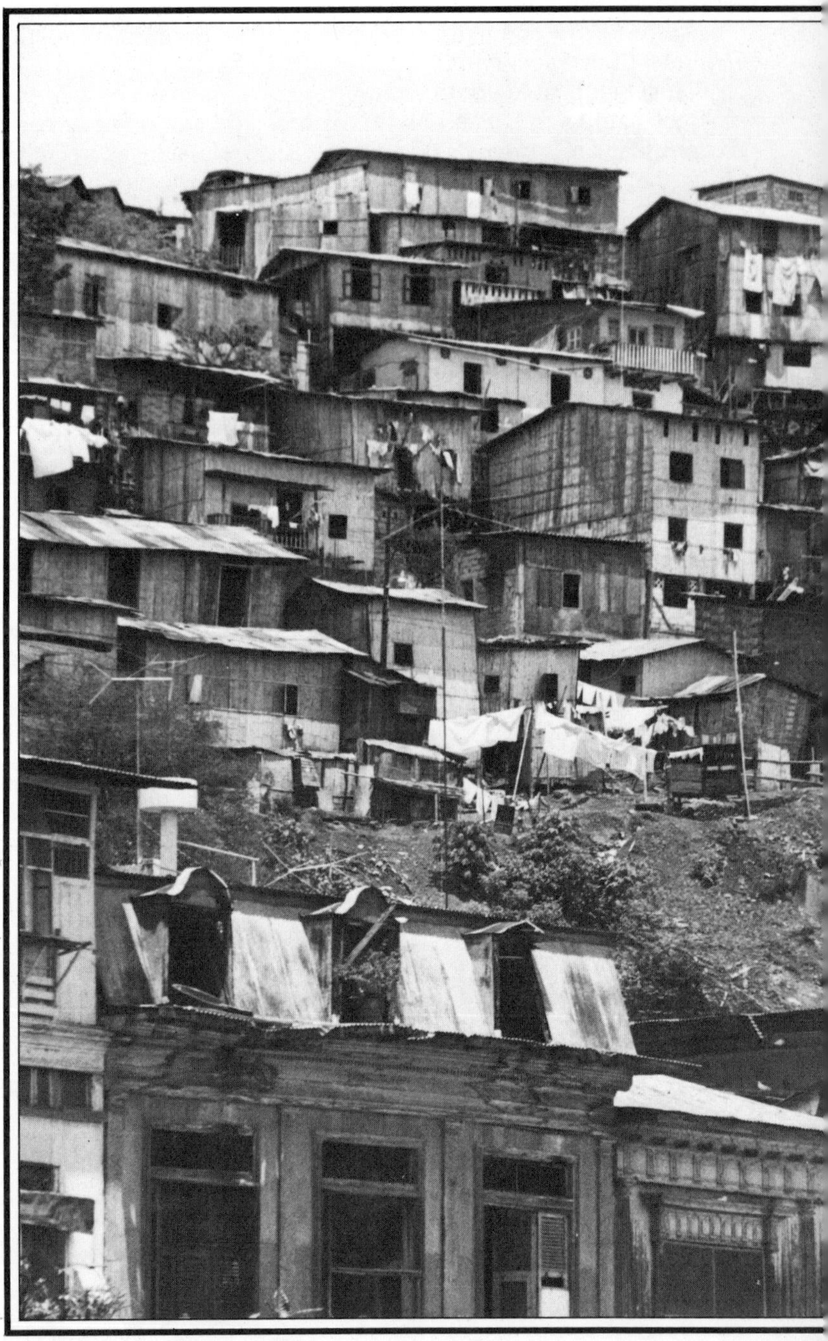

*Coping with
the Cities*

Chapter 5

Chapter 5
Coping with the Cities

IF YOU WERE an Indian from the Ecuadoran sierra just arrived in Quito to work as a laborer, porter, street vendor, or shoe shine boy, you might make your way to the street behind the Salesian Fathers' Don Bosco school, exchange greetings with the Indian women seated there on ponchos selling tomatoes, limes, beans, and spring onions, and enter a large, rambling wing of the school building that houses the Hospedería Campesina La Tola.

Inside you would find, as have over 13,500 Indians since 1974, a hostel offering a sleeping mat on the floor of a dormitory shared with other men from your community, hot showers, hot meals, a laundry, a volleyball court, workshops where you might learn a skill like carpentry or tailoring, and even a lawyer's office in case you run into a legal problem on the job. If you did not know about the hostel you would probably be sleeping on the sidewalk.

The hostel opened on New Year's Day 1974, but its origins go back to the previous year when theology students at the school started spending weekends in Indian communities in the sierra. Soon they noticed that they were running into some of the same Indians in Quito during the week, and that many of them were sleeping in the streets. They suggested the school make available some room in its large building, and the Salesian priests agreed. Then, like the servants in the parable, the students went out into the streets and roads to find guests. At the beginning, the hostel housed about thirty men. Now, more than three hundred can be found there at any time.

If you were one of these men, you could stay at the hostel indefinitely, although you would probably return frequently to your community, which you would still consider home, and to which you would return for good if you managed to solve the economic problems that drove you to Quito in the first place. Perhaps a sudden freeze destroyed your crops, and to feed your family this year you had to earn a salary. Or maybe it was your turn to sponsor the traditional community fiesta, an expensive honor but not one to be declined.

You would have to pay the hostel for the place to sleep, and the other services: three sucres (about two U.S. cents) for the night's lodging, ten sucres for meals, and similar sums for laundry or for health services. If the staff of the law office represented you in a dispute and recovered some money for you, part of it would go to them.

You would vote in dormitory elections for a president, you would have to help keep the hostel clean, and you might wind up being responsible for admitting new guests, or for the storeroom where personal belongings are safeguarded, or for some of the other duties necessary to keep the place functioning. There would be Mass on Sunday night, which is not obligatory, although the general meeting after it is, and there you would see Father Pio Baschirroto—Padre Pio—leading the discussion of any problems that might have come up during the week.

Padre Pio is a burly, bearded priest from northern Italy, near Venice. Ordained in 1970, he first went to Ecuador two years later for a four-month stint with a group of Italian volunteers. "I fell in love with the people here," he said, "and I promised to return." The next year he did, and he has worked in the highlands of Ecuador ever since. In 1979, he took over the hostel.

"When the hospedería began," Padre Pio said, "it was just assistance, responding to all those migrants who were sleeping in the streets. As we went on, the idea developed of giving something more than just shelter, of thinking about education and training, literacy, workshop skills, and also about health and dental services and legal aid. All of this work is staffed by volunteers, except for the legal department: a full-time lawyer and several law students. That is what the Inter-American Foundation supports. It is the best and most important work that we are doing, and, without the Foundation, we simply would not be doing it."

For Padre Pio, the legal work is important for several reasons. First, it helps the Indians who come to the hostel. "We handle mainly labor cases here in Quito, where we've helped to halt the exploitation of the Indian," said Padre Pio. "Before, they often were cheated on their pay. Now, we've noticed that some of the foremen in the construction industry make sure the workers from the hospedería are paid. Second, it gives us a way to be in touch with the communities they come from. In 1970, one of the bishops set up a credit agency for peasant organizations that now has regional branches throughout the country. Our legal office works through them and receives cases from them, so we're reaching the whole country. Those are more complicated cases: water rights and land and boundary disputes. Finally, our legal work is having a growing impact on the national legal system. We have two branch offices now and are thinking of opening two more. But most important is the formation of the law students working in the program, the education and experience and the commitment they are developing. I'm sure that even when the Foundation funding ends, these people, one way or another, will find a way to continue doing this work, and I think the organizations that are receiving the legal aid will find ways to support them financially."

Development and Dignity

All over Latin America and the Caribbean, people from the countryside are being forced into the cities by some of the same pressures that send Indians to the Hospedería Campesina. The Indians are atypical in that many of them will return to their traditional communities. The hostel has provided thousands of them a temporary solution to the first and most basic problems they encounter upon arriving in the city. But most migrants have made a more definitive break with rural life and need solutions more permanent than a hostel.

Roofs over Their Heads

For families everywhere, solving the problem of housing is usually the most expensive challenge they face. The migrants to Latin American and Caribbean cities often face that challenge with few resources beyond the strength of their backs, the skill of their hands, and the fact that so many other people share the same desperate need for shelter. Throughout the region, the need for housing has far outpaced the ability of either the government or the private construction industry to meet it.

The "organized" solution to the housing problem is normally some type of self-help project in which an agency supplies land, technical assistance, and materials, while the future residents do most of the labor. But the "irregular" solution of squatter settlements is more common. A few homeless families filter onto a piece of empty land on the city's outskirts and begin to live under a tent or tarpaulin. Gradually they are joined by others in a process of slow encroachment, and, before long, there is a settlement. Or, people organize by the hundreds, swoop down on a vacant lot, and throw up flimsy shelters out of whatever materials they have been able to find—sticks, cardboard, flattened tin cans. If they are lucky, they somehow withstand the first attempts by the police to dislodge them, and with each day that passes, the new community takes on a bit more permanence. In most cities, there are fairly substantial neighborhoods boasting houses of concrete blocks and normal municipal services that began years or decades ago with a midnight invasion of unused land.

Over the years, the Inter-American Foundation has sought ways to support people in their struggle for housing. It has directly backed some twenty cooperative construction projects. In 1972, it funded the Fundación Salvadoreña de Desarrollo y Vivienda Mínima (FUNDASAL) in a major self-help construction program. The success of that program subsequently attracted much larger financing from the World Bank and resulted in one of the largest private low-income housing efforts in Central America. In 1986, with Foundation support, a group of Kuna Indians were building 240 cement-block houses at the end of a dirt road about a half-hour bus ride from Panama City. The Indians, who live in the slums of Panama City and Colón, work holidays and weekends at the site, which they have named Dule Nega (House of the Kuna).

But the need for housing in the region is so enormous and the Foundation is too small to make much of a dent by direct support for construction. Instead, it has tended to respond to initiatives in housing that test new designs and approaches to low-cost construction, and especially to those that promise to strengthen community organizations to tackle the problem on their own. As the experience of squatter settlements shows, people's capacity for organization and joint effort, once mobilized, is the major resource in the struggle for housing.

Two projects currently funded by the Foundation, one in Chile, the other in Colombia, grew out of preliminary studies into just how squatters and people in poor neighborhoods organize, or fail to organize, to solve their housing problems.

Technicians without Ponchos

CIPMA, the Centro de Investigación y Planificación del Medio Ambiente (Center for Investigation and Planning on the Environment), is a group of architects, lawyers, economists, sociologists, and urban planners who began to meet as a discussion group at the University of Chile in 1979. Looking for a way to help with the serious housing problems in the poorer neighborhoods of Santiago, Chile's sprawling capital city, they decided they first needed to know exactly what the people there were already doing.

They found that families usually relied on their own scant resources to solve their most pressing problems, for they could expect little assistance from the government. They built or improved their own houses, for example, with little or no assistance from their neighbors, and with very little sharing of information or techniques. To the professionals' eyes, the process was economically inefficient, and the result technically deficient.

However, sometimes they banded together. They would cooperate on such projects as buying food in bulk to save money or on the *olla común* or common pot, when food was extremely scarce. They would band together, finding security in numbers, in the face of an outside threat or to present a petition for help to government or church authorities. But in general, the researchers found organizations to be weak in the neighborhoods they studied. Even in those communities born of a highly-organized land invasion, they found that, once the initial urgency had passed, interest in joint activities waned or disappeared altogether.

Development and Dignity

The professionals saw several ways to improve and strengthen the survival mechanisms the people employed and to solve many of the technical problems they were encountering. But they hesitated to introduce their solutions in a way that might undermine some of the positive characteristics they had also found in the poor neighborhoods, above all the people's sense of self-reliance. They began to work out a way to contribute their technical skills to poor neighborhoods that would not threaten that self-reliance.They wanted to be facilitators, not the traditional university-trained professionals who impose their ideas on poor people.

The CIPMA team decided that for their technical assistance to produce benefits for a community, the first priority had to be strengthening the grassroots organizations. "We wouldn't get anywhere making suggestions on how to improve housing construction or general conditions in the neighborhoods, if the organizations there weren't capable of implementing them," Eduardo Walker explained. Walker, a young architect, took the CIPMA approach into one of the neighborhoods the group had looked at—Nuevo Amanecer, a community of some five hundred families living on land rising gradually toward the mountains in the municipality of La Florida on Santiago's eastern flank.

During the presidency of Salvador Allende (1970-1973), this community, then known as Nueva La Habana, was politically organized and vocal in its support of Allende's "transition to socialism." So it suffered particularly in the repression after a military junta overthrew Allende in the violent coup of September 1973. For the next ten years, the residents of the renamed neighborhood lived under the watchful eyes of representatives of the military government. Even their own neighborhood leaders were named by the municipality.

By 1984, however, both the residents of Nuevo Amanecer and the CIPMA team saw possibilities for new initiatives. The people had run out of patience with the leaders appointed for them. The mayor of La Florida was open to the idea of the neighborhood people organizing themselves for self-help efforts. And there was a fund of 400,000 pesos due the families of the community from Operación Invierno (Operation Winter), a government program of minimal disaster relief to the poorer neighborhoods of Santiago that are frequently flooded by winter rains.

Having elected their own leaders for the first time in a decade, the people of Nuevo Amanecer met to consider what to do with the 400,000 pesos. Previously, disaster relief funds had been divided among heads of households. "Normally, that kind of money goes into a community, is divided up, and disappears like water," Walker said. In this case, the community requested the money in a lump sum, and invested it in a "bank" of construction materials that they were able to buy at the prices building contractors paid. The materials, mainly wood and cement at first, were "lent" out to the families that needed them. By now, about half the families in the community have taken out such loans. Repayment is in cash, with interest, allowing the bank to replenish its stock and to put profits into other community activities.

CIPMA, meanwhile, was coordinating a series of training sessions requested by the community on such topics as literacy, first aid, preventive health, and the manual skills of shoemaking, tailoring, weaving, carpentry, barbering, vegetable gardening, and raising rabbits. The courses promptly led to small projects in most of those areas, including a community newspaper. Profits from the construction materials bank provided initial capital. The bank also subsidized bread and milk for the community's child care center.

The community set up a commission to handle each of its new activities, encouraging a decentralization of authority and a sharing of responsibility favored by its newly-elected leaders. Working with the appropriate commissions, Walker and the other CIPMA professionals supplied the technical advice needed as the people moved to solve long-standing problems: improving their housing, stringing electrical cables safely, building a community center, putting in sidewalks, and improving drainage to forestall future winter floods.

In the process, the community and the professionals have created a new sort of partnership, one Walker thinks will endure. "We're going to continue working there," he said. "We've got a commitment to those people. It's important to us that we've gained their confidence, and we want to keep it." To the community, Walker and the CIPMA team are a new experience. "We were used to *los tecnicos de poncho*," one of the community leaders said. "Those experts who put on a poncho to show they're just like us. They come out when there's an emergency, stand around and give orders about what needs to be done, and then you never see them again. Eduardo is different. He's not talking down to us. With him, it's a horizontal relationship."

A Contagious Sense of Responsibility

Thousands of miles to the north, in Bogotá, Colombia, is another Foundation-supported housing project that also grew out of a concern about the proper relationship between professionals and the people they profess to serve.

For several years, Carlos Morales, dean of the architecture school at the University of Los Andes, has taught a course on low-cost housing. He invites leaders from poor neighborhoods to help him teach it and often holds the classes in those neighborhoods, not at the university campus. "The academic world creates an image of

Colombia that is divorced from the true reality," Morales said. "I want my students to see that reality. I'm also trying to get across to them the importance of a sense of service, a sense of responsibility as professionals. You can't teach it. It's passed on. It's contagious. But in working with students, trying to get them involved, there's a fine line. There's the risk of terrible attacks of charity. That's not what I'm after."

Ten years ago, Morales's contagious sense of professional responsibility was caught by three of the students in his course on low-cost housing, among them Patricio Wills. They did field research on self-help housing efforts in communities around Pereira in Viejo Caldas, west of Bogotá. Like their Chilean counterparts in CIPMA, they found both high levels of group participation and an often irrational use of human and technical resources. They saw that an organization providing advice and technical assistance could make an important contribution. They told Morales of their interest in starting such an organization, to be called CECA, the Centro de Estudios Comunitarios Aplicados. He put them in touch with Inter-American Foundation representative Marion Ritchey Vance. "It was the conversation with Marion that turned what had been only a theoretical idea into something practical," Wills said. "It was because of the enthusiasm of those students," Morales added, "that the Foundation funded CECA."

Like the CIPMA team, CECA's architects concluded that organization was the key to progress in a community. They began work by subsidizing local leaders from the neighborhoods so that they could devote full-time to organizing. As the communities got better organized, their determination to solve their housing problems grew, and the CECA team members, which soon included sociologists, psychologists, economists, lawyers, and social workers, began to offer their specialized knowledge. Eventually, they were assisting self-help housing projects for 380 families in eight separate communities. "When we felt things were functioning well," Wills said, "we moved the program to Bogotá."

Bogotá proved a larger challenge, mainly because the communal traditions still strong in small communities are much less evident there. But Bogotá is also where the problems of rapid urbanization are most sorely felt. Its population has exploded in the last three decades from under 700,000 to almost five million. In such a situation, as Carlos Morales points out, self-help construction is the only real possibility for most people seeking housing.

In 1979, CECA began to work with groups of low-income families aspiring to own their own homes. One such group, Los Comuneros, in the San Cristóbal Norte section of Bogotá, started with thirty-six members, linked because they all had children in the neighborhood nursery. The membership soon grew to over 150. All agreed to participate in a monthly savings plan that within two years made them eligible for enough credit to buy the land where they would eventually build their own houses.

In its work with such groups, CECA contributes advice and technical assistance on legal and financial matters and coordinates training in the necessary construction skills. But its chief priority is always to strengthen community organizations. "We see housing as a means, not the final goal," Patricio Wills said. "The final goal is a series of concepts, a philosophy, that will equip them for other things." His former mentor, Carlos Morales, argued the same point. The self-help approach to housing, he said, "should not be seen as an isolated solution. It implies the need to work in the community and to participate in matters that go beyond simply doing manual labor. It implies discussion and training and suggests that the solution to an immediate problem—the need for housing—can help solve other community problems, such as health, education, or generating additional income."

Making a Living in the Cities

Cities are marketplaces. Except for those few created for political or ceremonial functions, most of the world's cities grew up to satisfy the needs of commerce. They are centers of economic activity, and the hope of finding a niche somewhere in all that buying and selling of goods and services is one of the strongest magnets pulling rural people to the cities. But in recent decades, cities in Latin America and the Caribbean have grown faster than national economies, and alarmingly high levels of unemployment afflict their poorer neighborhoods. In response, people have come up with a variety of ways to make a living, and private groups with a sense of social responsibility have devised ways of assisting them.

In line with the belief that shelter is only one of the problems poor people in cities face, the CECA team in Bogotá has recently begun looking beyond housing projects to the economic life of urban neighborhoods. It seems fitting that, given the central role of the marketplace in cities, their glance fell first on the market of La Perseverancia, in a crowded working class neighborhood not far from the bullring, and almost in the shadow of the modern skyscrapers of downtown Bogotá.

The market, a large, square building housing permanent stalls with an open space behind it where peasants used to bring their produce on Saturdays, opened in 1944. Since then almost no improvements have been made, and the place has been very poorly maintained. As a result, the facility has deteriorated badly. There are serious sanitation

Development and Dignity

and garbage removal problems, poor drainage, and crowding. Over the years, many of the peasants who sold fruits and vegetables in the open patio behind the market building on Saturdays became permanent shopkeepers *(puesteros)*, but their stalls, built of scrap wood, tin cans, pieces of cardboard, and sheets of plastic, still retain the ramshackle look of a squatter settlement.

The market is run by a government agency, but rights to stall space, both inside and out, are passed down within families. The agency collects rent from the ninety-six puesteros but has done no planning. One result is that the market has become an unappealing jumble. A second is that most puesteros barely make enough to survive and pay rent.

Although they work almost elbow to elbow in the crowded patio, the puesteros rarely coordinate their efforts. For example, most of them sell the same items, but they buy their produce independently. "In three months," CECA director Clemencia Escallón said, "just by pooling their transport costs, they could buy a truck."

But just as the CECA team sees positive values in the poor residential neighborhoods where they work on housing, so do they see patterns worth preserving and encouraging in La Perseverancia. Although it is only a few blocks from the big hotels and sleek shops and restaurants of downtown Bogotá, the market is the center of a more traditional city. Despite changes in Bogotá, the neighborhood has maintained its stability since workers from the brewery once located down the hill began to move in fifty years ago. Inside the market building, local people still congregate at the stalls serving hot food. They drink coffee or herbal tea, perhaps consume a steaming broth against the chill of the Bogotá morning, and visit, do business, and exchange news with their neighbors. Also, the market is indispensable for the neighborhood's poorer families who live a hand-to-mouth existence and buy their food each day only when the money for it has been earned. For people who buy one onion, a carrot, two potatoes, and a bone with a tassel of meat for the evening meal, Bogotá's modern supermarkets, where most items are already packaged in quantity in plastic bags, are as remote as the downtown jewelry shops selling emeralds.

CECA has begun a five-year plan of working with the puesteros and the local community organization. The first step was to offer literacy courses, followed by training in marketing and administrative skills. CECA's architects and planners can see many possibilities for transforming the market. It could be made more efficient and more profitable. Space could be redesigned for multiple uses so that, for example, part of the patio could serve as a neighborhood park at night. But CECA's approach is to concentrate first on the people. The organization is convinced that if it can help the puesteros improve their economic situation and acquire the skills they need to run the market themselves, the physical transformation will soon follow. If it does, what CECA learns in the process can be applied elsewhere. "This is a pilot project for us," Escallón said. "There are about twenty of these markets in Bogotá."

Hard-Hatted Women

Off Old Hope Road in Kingston, Jamaica, about a hundred construction workers swarmed over a building site where a thirty-six-unit apartment complex was going up. On the second floor, Millicent Powell carefully smoothed the wet cement around an electrical switch box. In the next building, across a muddy courtyard filled with scrap lumber, Asalee Bailey was framing in a window. They were the only two women on the job.

The economic role of women in traditional rural societies tends to be fairly circumscribed. Women work ceaselessly— raising children, doing all the household chores, and frequently working in the fields weeding and harvesting. But generally they go no farther. In the cities, however, the pressure on women often intensifies. In many cases, in addition to domestic duties, they must seek work outside the home. Frequently, they find themselves the only source of income for their families.

In Kingston, the Women's Construction Collective is trying to help poor women break out of the economic trap that limits them to low-wage jobs as domestics or unskilled workers in light industry. The collective gives them six weeks of training in construction skills, finds them their first job, and equips them with their first tools from a revolving credit fund that the women repay. "It started as a pilot project to show that women could do this kind of work," said Ruth McCloud of the Construction Resource and Development Centre, which began the collective. "The government was uninterested in training women."

She went on, "We began in a small way. I had done research on the construction industry and had a network of contacts. I would ring up a contractor and say, 'Look, would you take on some women? You don't even have to pay them at first. No obligation. Just try and see if they work out.' And they all kept them on." Women with jobs, like Millicent Powell and Asalee Bailey, now earn twice what they could as domestics or in light industry.

"Construction in Jamaica is a rough industry," McCloud continued. "A lot of it is patronage jobs from the politicians. There's a lot of violence. All our women come from the bottom, from the slums. They're tough enough to survive. And we've found that when women are on the job, violence goes down and productivity goes up."

Development and Dignity

But there aren't enough jobs open with contractors to place all the women, and the construction industry is subject to frequent layoffs because of economic contractions. In search of other opportunities, the collective began a home repair business and also joined in a program with the government's disaster preparedness office to upgrade housing in low-income, hurricane-prone areas of the country. And they are looking at another potential market for the women's skills in the renovation of old houses. "We've got an architect who's doing research, finding the old artisans and interviewing them about their techniques, the finishing work, the trim and moldings," McCloud said. "I think there's a big market here in Kingston in restoring some of these beautiful old houses. And the women have an advantage because they're good at that fine work. We want to get these old artisans to come and teach our women."

Meanwhile, according to McCloud, the women in the collective are changing in many ways. "The most important changes are not always visible. I'm saying after a year in the collective, a woman can now go to the bank and open an account. That, and the fact that she has construction skills, means a total change in her life. Most of our women, about 90 percent, are mothers. Unwanted pregnancies are a big problem. If they get pregnant while they're in the training program, they're out. It's only happened once in two years. And once they get a job, you find they no longer get pregnant by accident."

"It's new to Jamaica to see women doing this work," said Asalee Bailey, who is proud to be earning the same pay as men and plans to go into construction management. "It's new to me," said Millicent Powell, who worked in a food production plant before. "I like this better. It gives me confidence competing with men. Not one of them could finish that switch box like I just did."

Barrio Capitalists

A casual, first-time observer might see the slums of Latin American and Caribbean cities as sloughs of despond. A closer look however generally reveals a bustle of activity, especially economic activity. The front room of a flimsy house may serve as a neighborhood store, selling soap, cans of food, packages of noodles, and loose cigarettes from an open pack. From another house may come the aroma of baking bread or the tapping of a shoe repairman's hammer. A woman may be sitting in a doorway knitting a shawl. In a small cleared space behind the house, her husband might be making a bed frame with simple tools for a customer down the street. Though fenced in by all sorts of barriers, the entrepreneurial spirit is very much alive in the barrio.

In San José, Costa Rica, a group of business people, spurred on by a proselytizing visit from a representative of the U.S.-based Institute for International Development, has made credit and technical advice available to would-be barrio businesses. In 1984, the group, known as ADAPTE (Asociación de Ayuda al Pequeño Trabajador y Empresario—Association for Assisting the Small Worker and Business Person), received a grant from the Inter-American Foundation to expand its program. ADAPTE's president, Jaime Cabezas, runs the San José lumber yard and building supply business he inherited from his father. He describes himself as an evangelical Christian and a defender of the capitalist system, "the least bad system we've seen." He said he and other Protestant businessmen set up ADAPTE because "we think the best way to defend the traditions of Costa Rica is to encourage as many Costa Ricans as possible to be owners of something."

ADAPTE, with help from the Inter-American Foundation, offers a rotating credit fund to small businesses (one to five employees) lacking the collateral for bank loans. Its loans are usually for one to two years, at 20 percent interest. (Banks charge 26-32 percent; in 1985 inflation was running around 15 percent). Most of the loans have gone to small enterprises based on needlework, weaving, tailoring, shoe repair, baking, mechanics, auto body painting, and small-scale commerce.

ADAPTE does not advertise. People learn of it by word of mouth, manager Hernán Fernández explained, mainly through a network of Protestant pastors. "Yes, we do get a proportionate percentage of requests from the Protestant community," Fernández said. (Costa Rica is 80 percent Catholic.) "Some people here say we favor Protestants. But this is a strictly financial relationship. We don't refuse a person because of religion." About twenty loan requests come in each month. ADAPTE's staff screens them, checks the applicant's reputation with his references and neighbors, and if it approves, passes the application on for final approval to a volunteer credit commission, made up of experienced business people. About half the requests are approved, and ADAPTE had made about 150 loans by late 1985. Once a loan is approved, ADAPTE staff visit the client each month. "We try to be aware of problems as they come up," Fernández said. "We want to see that the investment plan is actually carried out."

Several of the loans have already been repaid. "Of the 150," Fernández said, "only nine have been bad loans. We always try to have some guarantee, and we will go to court if necessary when people refuse to pay. But we're flexible and we'll look for the easiest repayment schedule. The problem is that people are accustomed to donations. We're trying to change that mentality."

The Tricicleros of Santiago

A thousand miles across the Caribbean from Costa Rica, in the city of Santiago de los Caballeros, near the north coast of the Dominican

Development and Dignity

Republic, some 7,000 street vendors, called *tricicleros*, weave their tricycle-driven carts through the streets on their daily commercial rounds. Here too, a group of local business people have joined together to contribute to their region's progress. One of the results has been increasing independence and income for the tricicleros.

The story of almost every organization in the Dominican Republic begins with the assassination of Rafael Trujillo. For more than three decades, Trujillo ruled the Dominican Republic like a personal fiefdom. He controlled and exploited everything and everyone in the country and permitted no freedom. He viewed independent organizations as potential threats. When Trujillo died in a hail of bullets on a lonely highway in May 1961, the long-repressed energies of the Dominicans flowered. All over the country, civic, political, and cultural organizations sprang up. In Santiago, twelve business leaders, among them Jorge Blanco, later president of the nation, founded the Asociación para el Desarrollo (Association for Development), the first such group in the country. With the dictator gone, a new nation was being put together, and the leaders wanted the business sector to take a leading role in solving some of its problems.

In the quarter-century since, the association has been central to the development of the Cibao region. It opened the country's first commercial bank with local capital, as well as savings and loans institutions, which have sparked large housing projects, and other financial institutions providing capital for agricultural and industrial development. It has supported education, training, research, and cultural events. With support from the Inter-American Foundation, several of the group's projects have been directed at peasants in the Cibao. In recent years, the association has introduced new strains of goats, sheep, and donkeys to improve the livestock on peasant holdings. At the same time, the small business loan program has expanded to reach the poorest entrepreneurs.

Teófilo Ramos, father of six, is a construction worker trained to operate a machine that makes cement bricks, but he can make more money by selling goods from the tricycle-driven cart he has wheeled through the city for the past two years from six in the morning to five in the afternoon. Ramos used to rent the cart for 1.50 pesos (about 50 U.S. cents) a day, which in a year came to over 500 pesos. Then a group of organized street vendors told him about loans available from the association.

"We wanted to encourage them to organize, to form groups," said Julio Guillén, executive secretary of the association. "So we made the loans to small groups of street vendors rather than to individuals. Teófilo's group, San Nicolás, has six members. We lent them 2,400 pesos."

With the loan, the members of San Nicolás bought their own carts. Within a year, spending less than they would have for rent, they had repaid the loan. Now they have applied for a new loan for working capital. So far, the association has financed two hundred groups—about 1,500 street vendors—in the same fashion. Guillén said a recent study showed that 64 percent of the groups have been able to raise their income by 60 percent. "I'm very thankful for the loan," Ramos said. "With six children, my biggest problem is putting them through school."

Who's Watching the Kids?

One of the biggest problems for most people in an urban setting is taking care of their children. Children need shelter, food, clothing, education, play. In large cities all over the world, providing for those needs often surpasses the capabilities of the family and becomes society's responsibility. In many cases, society fails. Children suffer poor health and malnutrition, abuse, abandonment, and exploitation. They fall into delinquency, street crime, drug use. In some of the cities of Latin America and the Caribbean, these problems reach alarming proportions, and their victims are everywhere. In those same cities, some of the most imaginative solutions have been fashioned.

Gloria Torres has been working with church-sponsored human rights organizations since shortly after the violent military coup in Chile in 1973; first with the ecumenical Comité de Paz (Peace Committee) and then, when the Pinochet dictatorship closed that down, with the Vicaría de la Solidaridad (Vicariate of Solidarity), a branch of the Catholic Church. As a lawyer, she has participated in countless battles to protect people from the repression of the last thirteen years—the arbitrary arrests, the torture, the disappearances of prisoners without a trace; and from the consequences of the government's economic model—high unemployment and the elimination of or drastic cuts in social services. Right now, she heads the vicariate's teams in the *zona norte*, the northern part of the city of Santiago, in the community of Conchalí. One of the activities there that most excites her is a recreation program for children and youth planned and carried out by thirty-two local groups of parents and their neighbors.

"You have to understand how important recreation is for us," she said. "The central problem is hopelessness, resignation, fatalism. We're trying to inject a new hope, to show that in the midst of the surrounding terror, we can laugh."

Torres recalled the vicariate's various attempts to assist the people of the zona norte. "We organized job exchanges to help people find work. But there was no work. We had to close them. We worked on the problem of the disappeared prisoners. I personally must have submitted a thousand petitions for judicial protection for prisoners, and not one was effective. What we were giving the people was yet one more experience of failure. We needed something that would succeed, something that didn't depend on anything beyond the resources that they had within themselves, that depended only on their solidarity and their capacity to organize. So we decided to do something for the children, and we began to prepare the neighborhood, the parents, the youth, and the children for an experience that united the whole community."

The idea was to provide a summer camp for the children of the neighborhood between the ages of three and eleven. January and February are the summer months in Chile, when the rich and the middle class abandon Santiago for the Pacific beaches or the lakes and mountains of the south. Conchalí mobilized to give its children a week's vacation from its hot, dusty, summertime streets. Local merchants contributed many of the necessary supplies. Parents scoured the barrio for anything that might help. Teenagers worked as camp counselors. The Archdiocese of Santiago provided a retreat house. For six days, there were games to play, songs to learn, water to splash in, and meals to share.

"We started with the children," Torres said. "We were looking for simple things to do: play, teach hygiene. We invited the teenagers to help. The focus was still on the children, but by participating, the teenagers found their own experiences, and our focus started to shift to include them as well. Now we're trying to figure out what to do next with the teenagers, as they grow up and develop new concerns. We see the need for some sort of cultural center, for sports."

The program has been in operation since 1981. In addition to the summer camps, each child can take part in at least one day's recreation each month during the rest of the year.

"The people worked hard to make this possible," Torres said. "And it has succeeded. It's an open, legal, public activity, something that the people here can come to, without the fear that surrounds so many other activities. And they can see the kids playing. The results are concrete. We don't think this is just a pastime, a way to escape reality. Rather, it better prepares the children, and everyone who participates, to stand on their own feet. We see it in the teenagers. They are more questioning now about their own future, their own reality. And in the process, we've rediscovered the importance of doing things as a group. Not just because it's efficient, but because it's good in itself. *Lo pasamos bien.* We enjoy it."

On Seventh Avenue

La Séptima is one of Bogotá's principal avenues, a broad street choked with traffic all day and into the night. Only in the early morning hours is it quiet. Quiet, but not deserted. All through the downtown area, the foolhardy pedestrian out after midnight can see the gamins, Bogotá's famous street urchins, searching for food, sharing a cigarette butt or some marijuana, or sleeping huddled together for warmth under rags in the scant shelter of a store's entrance. If the pedestrian is lucky, he may make it back to his hotel wondering why someone doesn't do something for those homeless kids. If he isn't, he may turn a corner and suddenly be jostled by a laughing, frolicking pack of gamins who vanish like smoke just as he notices that his wrist is scratched and his watch is gone. Then he will sputter furiously back to his hotel wishing the police would use their nightsticks and rid the city of those little hoodlums.

Far to the northwest, almost to Colombia's border with Panama, just down the palm-lined Caribbean beach from the sleepy town of Acandí, there's another thoroughfare known as La Séptima. This one is a concrete footpath two feet wide and raised about a foot above the muddy ground. It runs a few hundred yards from a cluster of whitewashed cement-block buildings out past the large vegetable garden to the corral where the cattle are sheltered for the night. The path was christened "La Séptima" with wry humor by some of the first gamins who came to this isolated jungle coast to carve out a new settlement and perhaps a new life for themselves.

The man principally responsible for taking hundreds of kids off Bogotá's Seventh Avenue and putting them on the jungle footpath is another Italian Salesian priest, Javier de Nicoló. Padre Javier grew up in a poor family in southern Italy. "My father was wounded in the First World War but never received a pension. He died when I was three, and our poverty increased. We lived in Naples, and I knew street kids there, but my mother saw that I got an education, and I grew up in a religious environment."

Sent to Colombia, Padre Javier was assigned to work with poor children. "But I was critical of the kind of Christian education we were giving them. It was too obligatory; it didn't respect the liberty of the individual. I became very critical, and in turn I was criticized for talking so much but not doing anything. That wounded my self-esteem. I began to work with kids in the jails and there I discovered something: that the bad child was made so by his society. A kid arriving in jail would be beaten by the others, robbed, and raped, but the moment he picks up a stick to defend himself, society says he's violent. I watched these kids entering and leaving the jails, and I said what's the point of working with the kids here? Why not work with them on the streets before they get here? At the same time, I learned that you could trust them. Once, on a bet, I took thirty kids from jail for a day's outing. We went all over and wound up in the best movie theatre in Bogotá. After the movie, three of them tried

Development and Dignity

to walk away. The other twenty-seven surrounded them. 'We'll help you escape later, but not now,' they said. And I returned to the jail with all thirty."

That trust became the rock upon which Padre Javier and the gamins built a unique enclave in the harsh world of the urban streets. What started in the early 1970s in Bogotá as an experiment to provide academic and technical training to gamins entering the program voluntarily, has now been duplicated in several widely-scattered areas of Colombia. The center for gamins consists of a special school that offers a high school diploma and workshop training. Those who decide to study join the community of La Florida, on Bogotá's outskirts. There they elect their own government, police themselves, play in their own symphony orchestra, run their own store, cafeteria, and bank, even have their own currency. Many of the graduates of the program stay with it as instructors to the next generation of gamins.

Giovanni Ferrera is a lean, intense man in his early twenties. He directs the recently-opened center for gamins in Medellín, a city that has experienced explosive and disruptive growth in the past two decades and is now known as the capital of Colombia's drug trade. Medellín is still a bit new to Ferrera, but he connects quickly with its street kids. For eight years, he lived by his wits on Bogotá's streets, running with a gang of thirty kids, sleeping under a bridge. "I specialized in robbing watches," he said. "And I smoked a lot of dope." For the last fourteen years, he has been in Padre Javier's program, sporadically the first several years, like most of the gamins for whom the call of the streets lingers, and then with increasing commitment. His peers elected him mayor of La Florida. Before taking the Medellín job, he ran the program's farm in Tolima, south of Bogotá.

"When I was on the streets, I was in and out of several institutions for kids," Ferrera said. "All of them were repressive. I rebelled. Gamins are rebels. We rebelled against our parents beating us at home, against the schools that despised us, and against the institutions that tried to make us conform." After spending several days at La Florida, Chilean novelist and poet Ariel Dorfman wrote that because they were rebels, the gamins should be a new kind of leader for Colombian institutions. "What Colombia has in this program," Dorfman said, "is a veritable human treasure. These children fled not only the inferno of their parents' homes but also a preordained and limited future. They dared to change their lives. . . . These are the most rebellious, critical, anti-authoritarian, adventuresome, self-reliant human beings that the Colombian poor could generate. In theory, they should be able to inject a much-needed vitality and wisdom into Colombian society."

Ferrera agrees that the gamins have much to offer and that, rather than their conforming to society, society should learn from them.

Coping with the Cities

"You've seen that we don't have any psychologists or any social workers in this program," he said. "That's because the kids are not the problem."

Perhaps the best way to be convinced of that is to leave Bogotá's mean streets and journey to the other Seventh Avenue, that concrete footpath in the jungle at Acandí. Up there, the kids are no longer called gamins, but rather *chilingos,* a name the local people, reminded of sandpipers scurrying around the beach in little flocks, gave them. The name is apt, not only because they are always on the move in bunches, busy as birds at something—football, construction work, electrical wiring, clearing land, basketball, climbing for coconuts, swimming, or a hundred other activities—but because of their transformation from street-smart urchins to confident pioneers on an isolated shore.

When the first gamins landed at Acandí about five years ago, there were just two small houses near the beach. The jungle rose up behind the line of palm trees. Everything to sustain the settlement had to be brought in by boat across the treacherous Gulf of Urabá. Several gamins and one of Padre Javier's colleagues, Father Alfredo Gómez, drowned when a boat was swamped in a storm in 1981. "He took more than two hundred boys up there, ones who hadn't passed through the program but had come almost directly from the streets," Padre Javier said. "He told me, shortly before he died, that the atmosphere in Acandí changed the kids. That it was excellent therapy for them. That's one of the reasons we persevered there."

Five years of perseverence and hard work have produced an impressive infrastructure. Neat paths bordered with ornamental plants connect the widely-spaced dormitories, classrooms, staff quarters, kitchen, and large, open-air dining room, where the chilingos gather for meetings and entertainment as well as for meals. Almost all the buildings are decorated with vivid murals in varied themes and styles, all done by an ex-gamin artist, Alejandro Gil. A gas generator provides electricity until lights-out at 10 p.m. Two football fields have been cleared between the kitchen and the beach, and a well-lit cement basketball court abuts one dormitory. From this complex, La Séptima leads off toward the vegetable garden and the livestock area (containing some ninety head of cattle and a few dozen chickens, with more to come). Beyond that is a circular road through the jungle that connects some fifty hectares of cleared land already producing bananas, plantains, avocados, guavas, corn, and pineapples. Eighty hectares more have been cleared for pasture. Along another road, which leads to Maniburro, there are plantations of fruit trees. Maniburro is a beautiful little cove with a gray sand beach where the chilingos swim on Sundays. Eventually, a port serving both the community and the town of Acandí will be built there. "The fruit will be for us and also

Development and Dignity

for the birds," one of the chilingos explained. "Since we've cut back so many trees, we have to think about providing something for the birds we've forced to move."

The chilingos take turns at all the work there is to be done at Acandí, but the main focus of the program there, in addition to regular academic classes, is to teach agricultural and construction skills. The chilingos rise at dawn, wash up, and go directly to their academic classes. They breakfast around eight and then divide up into work gangs for the morning tasks, either working the land under the direction of an agronomist or helping one of the manual arts teachers on a construction project. One morning in October, dozens of chilingos wielding machetes were clearing a hillside to open up building sites for more dormitories. Eventually, the community will have space for a population of 1,500. A visitor wondered if city kids cutting brush would be worried about snakes and other creeping or crawling things, but not a single chilingo confessed concern. "*Cosa que mueva, a la olla,*" ("if it moves, we put it in the dinner pot"), one beaming twelve-year-old chirped, making his machete go snicker-snack.

For most of the chilingos, despite the busy schedule of school and work, Acandí is an exhilarating break from the violence, hustling, and hunger they have known most of their lives. Free from the tension of the streets, they become children again, curious and rambunctious and shy by turns. A visitor walking around the settlement will eventually be approached by every one of them during the day. They will welcome him to the camp and ask if he slept well or if the mosquitoes bit him. He will have shaken hands with each one, and, at the end of the day, his watch will still sit safely on his wrist.

But when the months at Acandí are over, the chilingos go south again, back to the cities. Many of them will return to classes and workshops at La Florida. When they graduate they will have to face the daunting challenges of Colombia's large cities where housing is scarce, jobs few, pay low. Those urban problems will have to be solved in the urban centers. But Acandí, in addition to its character-building contribution to the gamins who pass through there, opens another possibility as well: a self-sufficient agricultural community where someday hundreds of gamins may settle, work productively, and raise their own children, who will not remember why the footpath past the old garden is called "La Séptima."

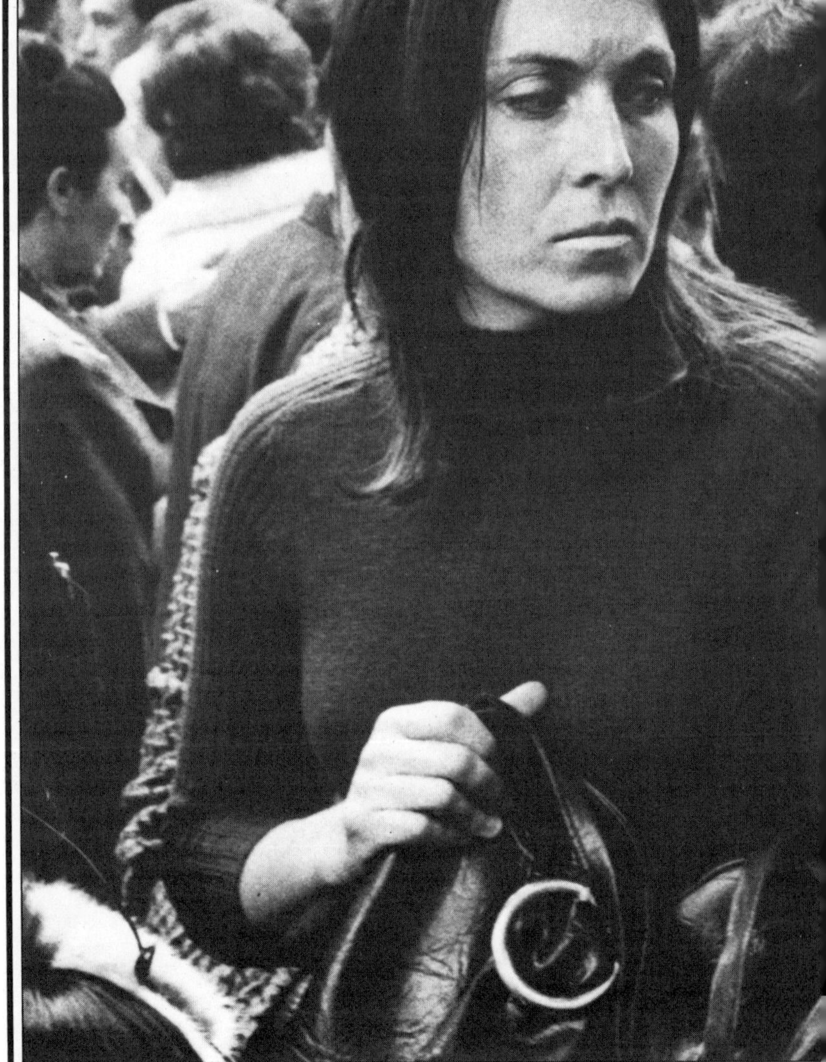

*Islands of
Democracy*

Chapter 6

Chapter 6
Islands of Democracy

FROM THE BEGINNING, democratic values guided the Inter-American Foundation's approach to Latin America and the Caribbean. The Foundation was created out of the faith that the common people of the hemisphere possessed the talent and organizational skills to solve their own problems. A second article of faith was that the Foundation needed to carry out its activities as independently as possible from the short-term policy interests of the U.S. government. Congressman Dante Fascell and many of his colleagues had long been concerned that development efforts were frequently interrupted or distorted when the regime of a country changed or when U.S. policy toward a regime shifted.

Events in the tapering end of the South American continent soon tested the Foundation's commitment to democratic values and its ability to act independently of the U.S. government. In the 1970s, when the tanks came out in Argentina, Chile, and Uruguay, the military regimes that took power put democratic traditions in mortal danger. U.S. policy toward those regimes shifted often in the succeeding years, from outright support to veiled and sometimes open criticism and back again. During this period, the Foundation was faced with the challenge of demonstrating its commitment to democratic values in a sustained, dependable way. A good deal of the trust the Foundation enjoys in the region was earned during some of the darkest days in the history of the Southern Cone countries.

The first of the decade's three coups took place in June 1973 in Uruguay, a nation in which democratic traditions had been firmly rooted since early in the twentieth century. Three months later, Chile, which in successive presidential elections had veered from conservative to reformist to socialist civilian governments, saw its proud tradition of democratic government rent by a military takeover. That same year, the return of Juan Perón to Argentina produced widespread euphoria that soon turned to disillusion. The country entered another downward spiral climaxing in the military takeover of 1976.

By 1976, the countries of the Southern Cone shared a terrible fate. Radical changes in economic policies and the dismantling of much of the social welfare system had dramatic effects on the poor, on workers, and on peasants and farmers. At the same time, the military governments employed torture, murder, and abduction to destroy opponents and to create a climate of fear that precluded any protest or political activity.

The advent of these regimes posed special dangers for those attempting to work with the poor. Development efforts, unless they are totally paternalistic, necessarily involve some degree of organization and common action by the intended beneficiaries. But in the tightly-controlled military dictatorships of the Southern Cone, independent organization was often viewed with suspicion if not hostility. In the small spaces permitted, people struggled to preserve the institutions, attitudes, and practices they believed essential to a future return to democracy.

The Inter-American Foundation was still a fledgling and little-known institution when the Southern Cone countries fell under the military heel. But its assistance was sought as courageous people worked to create or preserve islands of democracy.

Human Rights

Despite the grim similarities among them, the challenges and the possibilities varied greatly in the three countries. "In Chile," said Robert Martínez Nogueira, an Argentine professional who has evaluated Foundation projects in all three countries, "the long tradition of local organizations permitted some of them to survive and others to be created. And the Foundation could work with them. In Argentina the Foundation did what it could during the military government, but Argentina is basically an authoritarian society that lacks democratic organizations. The challenge there was to *create* spaces for democratic values. Uruguay is a fundamentally democratic society. The challenge there, as in Chile, was to *preserve* space for democratic values."

When the Chilean military took power in the coup of September 11, 1973, Cardinal Raúl Silva Henríquez was the Archbishop of Santiago. As the violence and repression of the new government became apparent in the first days after the coup, Cardinal Silva joined with leaders of other churches in Chile to create an ecumenical Peace Committee that offered some human rights protection. Two years later, when the dictatorship of General Augusto Pinochet closed down the committee, Cardinal Silva moved its work, and many of its staff, under the protection of the Catholic Church by creating the Vicaría de la Solidaridad (Vicariate of Solidarity), an official arm of the Archdiocese of Santiago. Soon, the vicariate was providing legal, medical, and counseling services, publishing a newspaper, investigating and documenting human rights violations, running lunch programs for children, and backing attempts to preserve some of the economic and social gains Chilean workers and peasants had made under previous governments.

Development and Dignity

"Chile had a history of an activist government," Cardinal Silva said. "In 1973, that was suddenly withdrawn. The dictatorship destroyed all the democratic organizations, repressed all the grassroots organizations in the country. The Church had to defend itself and the workers. In the past, they had their own organizations to defend them. But now they didn't. And so the Church entered. If the Church hadn't defended them, no one would have."

The Inter-American Foundation backed the Cardinal's efforts with grants for legal work in both rural and urban areas. The Departamento Campesino, the vicariate's rural office, received $427,000 for a three-year program to provide legal aid and training to peasant organizations as well as legal representation for individual campesinos on a case-by-case basis. Another arm of the vicariate, Pastoral Obrera, received $149,000 for its efforts to provide similar services and legal support to urban workers. But the problems affecting Chile's poor went far beyond the legal arena. Under the pressures of the government's economic experiment, Chilean society was beginning to unravel. Tariff protection for Chilean industries was all but eliminated. Many businesses failed, and thousands of workers lost jobs. Thousands more had been fired from government ministries. Labor unions were dismantled, prices on basic necessities allowed to soar, and welfare programs abolished. Expensive imported consumer goods flooded the country.

Much of Chile's pain was expressed in a new and spontaneous art form. Political repression had forced the country's long and vibrant artistic tradition of social criticism and protest into exile or hiding. Popular singers were jailed or killed, art exhibitions prohibited, books burned. In their place, the Chilean poor invented the *arpilleras*, brightly colored 15-by-20-inch tapestries made of scraps of cloth cut from old dresses, tufts of wool, and snips of burlap, all sewn together to portray a scene. Sometimes a few words spelled out in thread explain the theme. Often it is self-explanatory. One of the most common images during the 1970s was a door barred shut. Over and over in the arpilleras, small groups of people confront doors closed against them: doors of factories closed to workers, doors of schools closed to children whose parents cannot afford the expensive uniforms required of pupils, doors of health clinics closed to the unemployed whose medical insurance card had lapsed the moment they lost their jobs, doors of the courts of justice closed to plaintiffs, doors of the airport closed to exiles wishing to return, doors of the congress closed since the day of the coup.

The vicariate encouraged the production of the arpilleras and helped to market them, providing a minimal level of employment and income for hundreds of Chileans, many of them women whose fathers, brothers, husbands, or sons had disappeared into the maw of secret police prisons. At the same time, it sought to alleviate some of the problems the arpilleras portrayed.

"I was trying to help reweave the social fabric of Chile," Cardinal Silva said. "This was at a time when the economic situation was grave. The government had opened Chile wide to foreign trade. It was a violent change which led to large numbers of bankruptcies and a radical rise in unemployment."

The Cardinal's first steps had been to respond to what was perceived as a temporary emergency. As the nature of the changes being imposed on Chile sunk in, he sought to move beyond the defense of human and legal rights to confront the economic crisis. In rural areas, the Church took the lead in forming large intermediary institutions to assist farmers by providing rural cooperatives with credit, technical assistance, and training. In urban areas, the Cardinal and a team of advisers launched efforts to save jobs by helping workers buy and run the small factories where they had been employed. Several worker self-managed industries already existed in Chile at the time of the coup. With the sudden increase in unemployment and then the wave of bankruptcies, church-related institutions stepped up their support of those enterprises and sought start-up capital for new ones.

"Many people had reservations about what we were trying to do," Cardinal Silva recalled. "But the Inter-American Foundation didn't. I had met Bill Dyal through a nephew of mine. I found him very capable of understanding what we were facing. I felt with him and the representatives of the Foundation that we were together in the discussion of the project. That it was a partnership, not a gift."

By the mid-1970s, Foundation funding in Chile reached $4 million, about half of it going to the rural sector and a third to the attempt to save industries and put them under worker management. Eventually the Foundation became the principal financial support of the worker self-management sector in Chile, a sector which at its height included sixty businesses with about 3,600 employees. Although a few of the businesses still survive, most eventually went under. They started with huge disadvantages. In most cases, workers were able to acquire control because the owners were about ready to shut down anyway in the face of overwhelming competition from the flood of imported goods that government policies permitted. Typically, the businesses were staggering under a burden of already-incurred debt which the new managers had to meet. Their equipment tended to be obsolete, further limiting their competitiveness.

The world-wide recession exacerbated the effects of government policies, and many of the institutions receiving Foundation support failed. The strategy of trying to preserve the gains made in the past by campesinos and workers could not overcome the impact of current government policies. The sudden removal of state subsidies brought

Development and Dignity

the collapse of scores of cooperatives. Many small farmers who had once benefited from agrarian reform sold out to larger neighbors. As bankruptcies decimated Chile's manufacturing sector, the failure of the self-managed firms brought down the financial and training institutions that had been set up to serve them.

Because many of the national-level attempts to confront the economic crisis failed, the Foundation intensified its support for Chilean institutions that were researching development opportunities. Gradually it arrived at a strategy of backing smaller, more diversified, regionally-dispersed projects. It continues to support the vicariate's myriad programs of training, education, self-help, small-scale production, recreation, and community development throughout the vast zones of urban poverty and to work with similar institutions in other parts of Chile.

While most of the ambitious, national-level efforts like the worker-run industries did not survive in the new economic environment, some observers still praise the efforts that were made. "With the appearance of the military government," said Luis Brahms of Santiago's CIDE—Centro de Investigación y Desarrollo de la Educación (Center for Research and Development in Education)—"other institutions, like the Church, had to take over much of what previous governments traditionally had done. With the help of the Foundation they were able to do it for a time. But the military government simply wasn't going to let those businesses survive. That doesn't mean the idea was bad. In spite of the failures, many grassroots organizations were strengthened, and many people who had the ability to develop a critical perspective—people who would otherwise have been forced to leave—were helped to stay in the country. Thus, a group of people that could think of alternatives and elaborate programs for the future were sustained. The same thing happened in Argentina, and now many of those people are playing important roles in a democratic government."

Spaces for Reflection

Oscar Yujnovsky is now a high-ranking official in Argentina's Foreign Ministry. During the military dictatorship, he directed two Foundation-supported projects aimed at the housing problem in Buenos Aires. "The idea was to learn about the strategies poor people use so that eventually government housing policy could be reformulated. We did small pilot studies of how to cope with the eradication of the *villas de emergencia* (urban squatter settlements) by the military government, as well as long-term studies of individual families who built their own housing. We provided them with assistance for improving their houses—better designs, better techniques. These weren't abstract studies. We were looking for concrete solutions."

Yujnovsky said the Foundation was searching for a role in Argentina during the military dictatorship. "The Foundation tended to scatter its efforts," he said, "and the overall impact was reduced. It supported many different projects, rather than concentrating on one particular area. But that may have been because an organization needs to go through many different experiences in order to learn. Also, the Foundation was very action-oriented. It pushed for concrete responses to problems when perhaps, given the situation at the time, that wasn't possible. But, in the end, it provided assistance without imposing any conditions and without ideological distinctions. It helped groups that were very diverse but which shared democratic values and were pursuing communal solutions. At that moment, under the military government, it was more important to preserve and strengthen institutions and people and permit reflection than to carry out projects."

A significant part of the reflection that went on in Argentina during the dark years of the military dictatorship took place at CEDES, the Centro de Estudios del Estado y Sociedad (Center for Studies of the State and Society). "We founded CEDES in 1975," its first director, Jorge Balán, said, "because there wasn't space in the universities to do social investigation. It was a crisis. There was a great deal of repression and persecution. CEDES was for people who wanted to study Argentina and who wanted to stay here."

Initial support for CEDES came from organizations in Europe. Support from the Foundation came more slowly. "There was a long process of conversations with Inter-American Foundation representatives, trying to see how they could help us within their framework," Balán said. "CEDES was strictly a center for study, and the Foundation was looking for projects that had some element of action to them," said Elizabeth Jelin, a senior researcher who has been at CEDES since the beginning. "And there was a period, especially in Argentina, when any kind of action was dangerous." "What finally emerged," said Marcelo Cavarozzi, the present director of CEDES, "was a low-profile attempt to aid grassroots groups not loved by the military government and academics who were interested in the problems of those groups. There were special difficulties for the Foundation. It had to work in an atmosphere of a repressive government and also of an anti-Americanism perhaps stronger here than in other countries, especially in intellectual circles."

Peter Bell, the Foundation's second president, "recognized the importance of research," according to Balán. "And although during those years there was much you couldn't safely study, we found things you could: health, education, and what happened to those people who had lived in the villas de miseria the government bulldozed. There were changes in the standard of living. The welfare state was deteriorating. How were poor people reacting? What sorts of orga-

Development and Dignity

nizations were appearing? Finally, the Foundation decided to fund several of these small scale studies. We were a group of researchers who wanted to stay in Argentina. The assistance enabled us to do that. At the same time, we were providing information about the reality and the problems and the forms of organization of the grassroots groups the Foundation was interested in helping."

The political atmosphere in Argentina began to change in 1982 as the failures of the military's economic policy became all too apparent. Those failures, in turn, would urge the tottering military leaders into a last desperate gamble to hold power, the invasion of the Malvinas, or Falkland Islands. When that turned into a fiasco, the military government was doomed. In the meantime, Argentines had begun to shake off their fear, and criticism had become possible again. CEDES was ready to join the debate. "By 1982-1983, we had a more ambitious program," Balán said. "We were putting out more publications. They were more openly critical. And we were reaching a bigger audience. All this was based on those studies we had already done. Then, in 1984, with the new government, we could provide information, and even people, to advise it."

Democracy in Practice

Across the Río de la Plata, in Uruguay, the Foundation's support for democratic values of necessity went through more traditional developmental channels. Under the military government Uruguay bore little resemblance, on the surface at least, to the nation that, for most of the twentieth century, had been an island of political stability and democracy, of advanced social legislation and a solidly-established middle class. During the mid-1970s, it gained the dubious distinction, according to Amnesty International, of having a higher proportion of its population imprisoned for political reasons than any other country on earth.

The military was able to maintain complete domination, not just because it was willing to use force, terror, and torture, but because it controlled every private institution. No meeting could be held without prior notification of the authorities. No organization—whether the board of directors of a corporation, or women weavers in an isolated rural district—could elect its own officers until the authorities approved the list of candidates. For most of the period of military rule, no organization attempting to defend human rights was allowed to exist in Uruguay.

Military control was tightest in urban areas, particularly in Montevideo. Attempts at organization there drew suspicion. In the countryside, depending on the attitudes of local authorities, there were some possibilities. "Organization building is the Foundation's niche

Islands of Democracy

in development," said Cindy Ferrin, long-time Foundation representative for Uruguay. "In Uruguay, we didn't help new organizations, but we helped existing ones take on new life or new activities. And particularly in the last decade, we helped them survive. Mainly we have supported small farmers. It was a strategy forced on us in a sense. Although we couldn't work in urban areas, we did feel comfortable with cooperatives in rural areas."

Many Uruguayans have long shared the Jeffersonian view that a class of small, independent farmers is an indispensable thread in a nation's democratic fabric. But during the 1970s, Uruguay's small farmers were buffeted by the military government's economic policies, especially the lowering of barriers against imports of cheap foreign food. Many farmers, watching their children leave to look for work in the city, feared for the survival of their way of life.

The Foundation directly supported rural cooperatives in Uruguay during the dictatorship and backed organizations that provided them with technical assistance. One of those was IPRU (Instituto de Promoción Económico-Social del Uruguay). IPRU's thirty professionals, including agronomists, accountants, legal advisers, and organizers, work throughout the country to encourage the self-help efforts of low-income groups. They try to assist groups at the early stages of their activities and then pull out. Several years ago, IPRU worked closely with the cooperative in Durazno described in Chapter Four. There, and throughout rural Uruguay, it assisted efforts to form cooperative stores, to diversify production, introduce new crops, improve marketing, and to encourage participation and democratic ways of solving problems. During the years of dictatorship, these rural groups provided one of the few opportunities for democratic participation. "We were the islands of democracy in Uruguay," said Julio Arrillaga, an official of the Durazno cooperative. "We always managed to have free elections." For Raúl Bidart, director of IPRU, the significance of the Foundation's efforts in Uruguay was that it supported "projects that in one way or another constituted an alternative to the dictatorship. Not a political alternative, tied to the parties, but a social and moral alternative—democratic organizations."

In some of the darkest moments for the Southern Cone nations, the Inter-American Foundation found that its policy of responsiveness required it to support heroic people struggling against a nightmare that threatened to engulf them and all they believed in. Obviously, there is no precise way to measure the contribution it made. What most clearly endures from those experiences is a sense of bonds forged. José Zalaquett is a Chilean lawyer who was forced into exile in 1975 when the Peace Committee was closed down. Until then, he had led the legal struggle to defend victims of the government's repression. Ever since, he has closely followed events in his country

Development and Dignity

and the work of the Vicaría de la Solidaridad, which took over for the Peace Committee. He has thought often about what support from the Inter-American Foundation meant to him and his embattled colleagues in Chile, as well as in Argentina and Uruguay.

"The fact that an outside institution like the Inter-American Foundation supported you was a lifeline. It's as simple as that. The resources kept you going. On top of that, they talked with you and had ideas, suggestions, valuable advice, and good questions that would help you improve your own ideas. Most important was their solidarity. Even if they couldn't mobilize the resources to get you out of jail or to solve some problem, it was important to know that there was an island of expertise out there about you and what you were trying to do. If we were islands of democracy in the midst of our countries, they were islands of knowledge and concern in the midst of theirs.

"The fact that it was an official government agency did wonders. People began to realize something about the United States that perhaps they hadn't before. The United States was always important for us. It was always there, frequently in an inimical way. But the fact that you could enter into dialogue with people from the officialdom of the United States and find them ready to talk, to understand, and to work together made us start relating to the United States in a different way."

PART THREE:
The Foundation's Niche

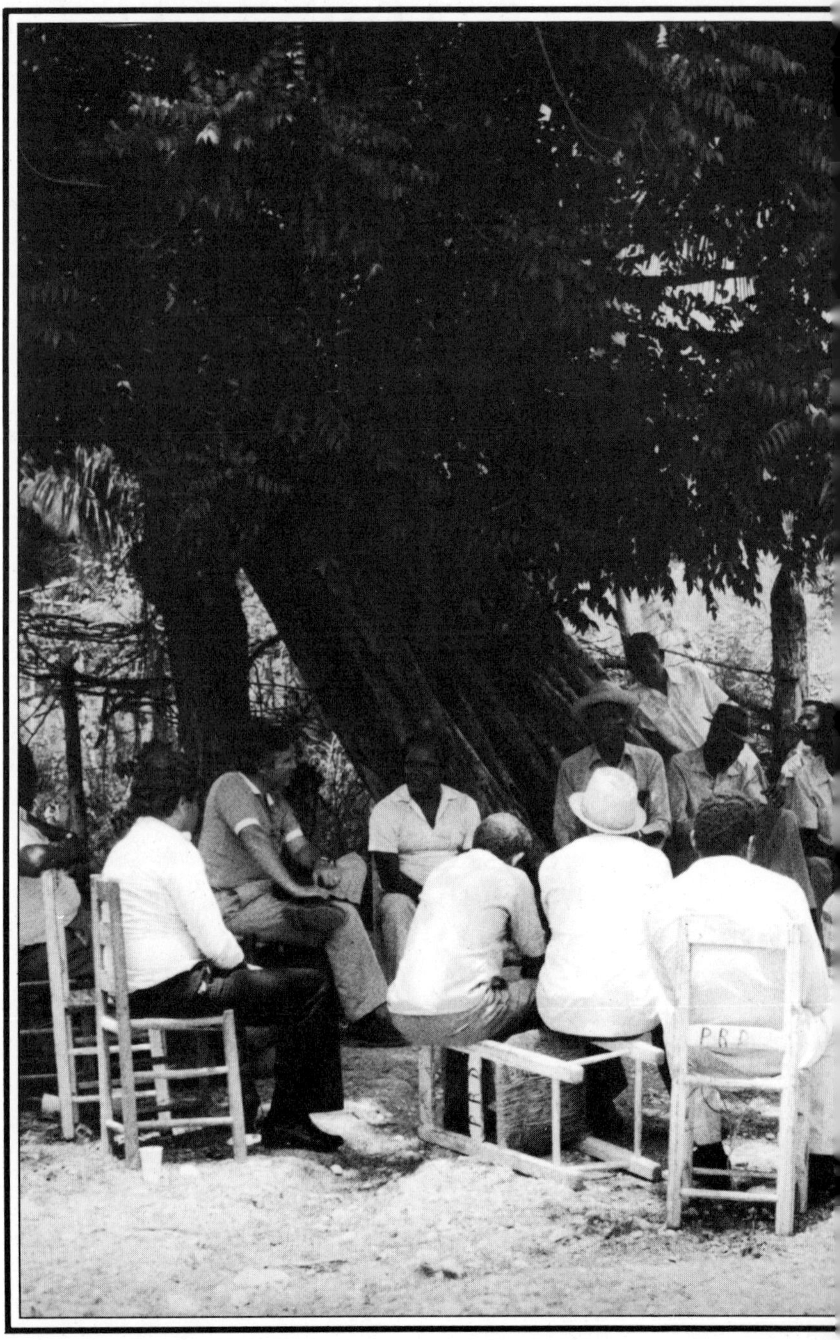
PRD

A Prophetic Institution

Chapter 7

Chapter 7
A Prophetic Institution

"AT THE HEART of the experiment which is the Inter-American Foundation," Lawrence Salmen, then a Foundation staff member, wrote in 1976, "is a vision of a new relationship evolving between the peoples of the United States and the Third World." The human impulse to share with those less fortunate had sparked many U.S. assistance efforts, both private and official, long before the Foundation appeared. But the Foundation put that impulse into practice in a way that opened up the possibility of a new vision. Describing her thoughts about the Foundation, a support staff member brought both the impulse and what was new about the Foundation together: "I grew up in Third World countries," she said. "I saw poverty through the eyes of a child, and I've never forgotten it. Working here is a way of being involved in improving the lives of people. But what's special about the Foundation," she continued, "what I saw when I had a chance to go into the field, was the way the representative, who is after all representing a superpower, can let the people there know that they are the managers of their own projects."

The Foundation's success in restraining the impulse to manage and control grew out of the decision that it be responsive. More than anything else, the posture of responsiveness gave the Foundation its unique nature, its special niche in development work. Making prompt decisions on funding requests, a preference for relatively small projects, and trying to get aid to the poorest people as directly as possible also characterize the Foundation, but other development institutions also follow such precepts. It is the posture of responsiveness that distinguishes the Foundation. Responsiveness allows the Foundation to express solidarity with the deprived peoples of the hemisphere and to express concern and sympathy while avoiding the pitfalls of charity and paternalism. It is what makes it possible for recipients to accept aid without losing their dignity. And that makes the Foundation, despite its limited resources, important both as a development agency and as a political symbol in the context of relationships between the United States and its neighbors in Latin America and the Caribbean.

The Foundation opened its doors, not by trumpeting a new crusade against underdevelopment, but by sending its representatives off simply to listen. Given the historical tendency of the United States to arrange matters for its neighbors, that approach bordered on the revolutionary.

A Prophetic Institution

Not only was the approach different. The freedom with which it was implemented, particularly during the first five years, was unparalleled for a government agency. This statement appeared in *They Know How*, a book the Foundation published to summarize the experience of those years: "The staff can confirm that every funding decision has been made without letting outside pressures influence it in the process, for or against." Such absolute freedom could not be claimed today. "Before," said a Foundation staff member, "when people reviewed a project, they talked about how it would affect the grantee. Now, sometimes, it's what will the President say, what will the board say, how will it affect our image with Congress? There was a project in Nicaragua a while ago. We never really talked about the project—just about the fact that it was in Nicaragua and how controversial it would be. I felt really demoralized when I walked out of that meeting."

"The freedom of the early years," said Charles Meyer, a member of the original board of directors, "was because of the wisdom of Dante Fascell and the other founding fathers in Congress." (The legislation creating the Foundation gave it $50 million. For the first five years, there was no need to return to Congress each year for appropriations.) "We could be apolitical until we had to start looking for money," Meyer said. Fascell had hoped to insure permanent independence for the Foundation by freeing it from the appropriations process. "I had permanent financing in the House bill," Fascell said. "But as a compromise with the Senate, we had to take that out. That's my only regret about the legislation."

Of course, the Foundation's independence in the first years was not automatic. "From day one," Bill Dyal wrote in the introduction to *They Know How*, "external battles have been fought to determine and preserve [the Foundation's] autonomy in decisionmaking and operations." Dyal recalled some of those struggles. "We had to face down incredibly angry ambassadors," he said. "We battled with members of Congress. Looking back, I may have been wrong to protect the staff from reality. I ran interference for them to leave them unencumbered to do their work. As a result they may think that everything was beautiful back then, because they weren't aware of the battles. It may have been too comfortable a place."

As the initial $50 million appropriation ran out, the Foundation, like other federal agencies, had to make its yearly case for funding to congressional committees. Inevitably, the Foundation became more controversial. By the end of the first decade, political winds had begun to swirl around it. Its operating style, its support for groups seeking change, its enviable freedom, all began to draw the fire of increasingly vociferous critics.

Development and Dignity

Struggle for the Foundation

Bill Dyal left the Inter-American Foundation in mid-1980, after nine years. "You get so wrapped up in an institution," he said. "I felt it was time for me to go." Peter Jones, a senior vice president and general counsel at Levi Strauss & Co., who had succeeded Gus Hart as the Foundation's board chairman two years before, directed the search for Dyal's replacement. The board's choice was Peter Bell, formerly the deputy under secretary at the Department of Health, Education, and Welfare, and before that, a veteran of ten years of work in Latin America and the Caribbean with the Ford Foundation.

"I wanted to shake the Foundation gently," Bell said, "without shaking its self-confidence. Its basic ethos needed not to be changed but nurtured. It was really a quite special agency within the government. The staff had a great respect for the people with whom they worked; they knew a great deal about the region and had strong social commitment. I felt that given the Foundation's achievements, there may have been too much defensiveness. There was an anti-intellectualism that wasn't totally misplaced, based as it was on suspicion of the validity of much of the research on social and economic development. I wanted to strengthen the staff professionally, and to reach out more to other parts of the larger development community. Above all, I wanted to challenge people to think critically and creatively. I thought that to work effectively at the grassroots level, we also had to involve people who could reflect on what we were doing."

But the shadow of increasing political pressure hung over Bell's tenure. "Even when Dyal was president," Bell said, "there were virulent critics. I met with them when I became president. They charged there was a 'Marxist-Leninist pattern' to our funding. I asked for examples. They had two, a newspaper in Costa Rica and a taxi drivers' union in Nicaragua supposedly run by the head of the Communist Party. It turned out to be a different person with the same name."

The critics were not appeased. Some questioned the Foundation's belief that very poor people know how to go about solving their problems—the philosophy of development that was summed up in the title, *They Know How*. Involve poor people in development projects, critics said, but don't put them in charge. Some critics challenged perhaps the central political characteristic of the Foundation since its inception, the idea that it should be independent of the short-term foreign policy interests of the administration in power. They wanted it brought into tune with U.S. foreign policy.

The growing pressures on the Foundation climaxed in December 1983 when a four to two majority of the board, all of them appointed by the Reagan Administration, fired Peter Bell. Seven months later, Deborah Szekely, a California community leader with forty years of experience as a businesswoman, much of it in Mexico, became the Foundation's third president. "I believed in what the Foundation was doing, and I thought it needed rescuing," Szekely said. "I thought I could save it." Her insistence on maintaining the Foundation's independence soon embroiled her in controversy as well.

These developments did not go unnoticed in Latin America and the Caribbean. Indeed, one indication of the importance many people in the region attach to the Foundation is the concern with which they have followed the debate over its future. The firing of Peter Bell, in particular, drew an outpouring of questions about which way the Foundation was headed.

In the view of many people in the hemisphere who know the Foundation, what its domestic critics find most objectionable about it goes to its very essence. To satisfy the critics would be to strip the Foundation of precisely the qualities hailed by people all over Latin America and the Caribbean.

In the charge that the Foundation has supported some groups on the political left, people in the region tend to see the old North American obsession with communism. For many of them, what has been most welcome about the Foundation is its openness and its interest in experimentation and development ideas that work. It is an attitude they find lacking in other official U.S. institutions.

"I'm struck by the blindness in your country," said Luis Brahms of CIDE, the educational organization in Chile. "It's a bit too myopic. The Foundation is completely atypical, compared to other U.S. agencies. Just for that reason alone, even those on the right should see the benefits of preserving it."

A variation on the left-wing bias charge is that the Foundation favors "collectivism" over free enterprise. But the Foundation's willingness to support organizations and group initiatives is one of the traits that has won it trust in the region. "In Latin America," said Raúl Bidart, director of IPRU, the institute that assists organizations such as farmer cooperatives throughout Uruguay, "we stress the group, the communal aspect. Maybe it comes from the Indian values, although Uruguay doesn't really have that influence, or from the Spanish, the Church, but it's an emphasis not on the material aspect of development but on the human. The Foundation understands this and accepts it. If this is what we stress, and if their philosophy is to respond to us, they have to accept it." Likewise, to abandon the principle that poor people should run their own projects would be to squander at a stroke the accomplishments of fifteen years. That principle is at the heart of the vast majority of non-governmental development initiatives in the region. From Haiti to Peru, Mexico to Patagonia, those initiatives

Development and Dignity

are based on the conviction that development is a subjective process, that it starts with and aims at the "empowerment" of the poor. Because the Foundation has respected and accepted that perspective, it has been able to work with various independent groups throughout the region in the close relationship that seems to be ruled out for any other official U.S. agency.

In pursuit of an illusionary coherence and efficiency in development projects, critics attacked the Foundation's flexibility, its willingness to change the design of a project in midstream. Yet flexibility is repeatedly mentioned as one of the Foundation's most welcome traits by people all over the region. The Foundation is flexible because it appreciates the often complex and shifting reality in which development projects are carried out. An appreciation for that reality comes out of the direct experience of development work at the grassroots level and probably can be gained in no other way. "The representatives were feeling their way, along with us, learning what development means in a context such as this," said Ronnie Thwaites, one of the founders of the Kingston Legal Aid Clinic in Jamaica. "They were willing to break some of the rules according to the circumstances."

Perhaps nowhere does the adage "if something can go wrong it will" so apply as in development projects. To deny the need for flexibility is simply to say you have never been there; that you have never waited weeks, with the ditches all dug and the pipes all laid, for a water pump to arrive, and then discovered it's the wrong horsepower; that you have never seen a sudden tropical storm wash out a newly planted field, Newcastle's disease destroy a chicken flock, or the mayor try to stack the leadership of a local community development group with party hacks. "The Foundation has introduced total flexibility into community development efforts," said Carlos Morales, dean of Los Andes architecture school in Bogotá and once director of Colombia's national community development agency. "It's an area that is usually so politicized. And the Foundation is very tolerant of political problems. It understands how political rivalry and mistrust affect projects and the need to be flexible if you're going to work in that area."

In recent years, what has most annoyed some critics is the perception that the Foundation acts independently of the short-term interests of the U.S. government. But from the beginning, the intent of the Foundation's creators was to establish that independence. "We knew the Foundation would have to gain trust to be effective," Congressman Dante Fascell said. "That's why we wanted to get it at least one step away from the U.S. government." Putting the Foundation under the control of a board of directors with a majority of non-governmental members was one way to establish that distance. Finally, the hard work of the Foundation's representatives over the years has been a major factor in building trust. In many countries, there was a great deal of suspicion about the Foundation when it first appeared.

"There's always the view that the Foundation is the agent of imperialism," Roberto Martínez said in Buenos Aires. "That view tends to change after contact with the Foundation. People learn that working with the Foundation doesn't mean they have to swallow any policy of the U.S. government."

"At the beginning, I was a bit skeptical," said Father Pio Baschirroto in Quito. "You know, doubts about whether this was related to the CIA and so on. So I was frank with the representative. There could be no political conditions, I said. Now, after four and a half years working with the Foundation, I've seen a real social concern on their part and no pressure."

As a result of its independence, the Foundation is perceived throughout the region as sincerely interested in the problems of development, with no hidden or not-so-hidden agenda of pushing short-term U.S. interests.

"When you compare it to other American institutions we've seen," said Father Pollux Byas, the Haitian priest who directs a development project around the community of Pilate in the mountains of northern Haiti, "the Foundation's efforts are for this country, and not for American interests. You can see that this organization is really autonomous. You feel at ease with the representatives, to say whatever you want."

Carlos Moreno, director of the development project that grew out of a literacy campaign among the Indians in the Chimborazo region of Ecuador, also saw the Foundation as an exception to U.S. institutions, which he said are frequently perceived as instruments of American control or paternalism. "The United States has tried to control the Third World in many ways," Moreno said. "And at the same time, it has tried to convey an improved image of the United States through technical assistance and development organizations. But they were all paternalistic. The Inter-American Foundation was based on the needs of the people. And it was created to be independent of the government."

In Colombia's Cauca Valley, peasant leader Gustavo Herrera said that when he and his colleagues first heard of the Inter-American Foundation, they were very cautious. "The coup in Chile, the overthrow of Allende was still very fresh," he said. "But with time we saw that the Foundation was incredibly autonomous and could permit us to maintain our own autonomy."

For Luis Brahms in Chile, "the appearance of the Foundation was like a shaft of light. It opened up the possibility of development efforts with U.S. support, but independent of the interests of the governments in power both here and in Washington. Because of the

Development and Dignity

hope the Foundation kindled, because it showed a more generous vision of the United States, we watched with some anguish the attempts to change it. That could not help but disturb us."

Lessons from the Struggle

The Foundation seems to have emerged from the period of struggle and upheaval that began prior to the firing of Peter Bell. During that period, it lost one president, and almost another. An attempt by members of the board to fire Deborah Szekely, the incumbent president, brought matters to a head in June 1985. It ended in a standoff, cooler heads eventually prevailed, and the dispute was patched up. "I think the Foundation has survived its strongest test to date," said Congressman Fascell.

Judging by dozens of conversations throughout the hemisphere, the years of controversy have not greatly affected the Foundation's work, nor its reputation, although concern about its ability to maintain its independence has increased. "I'm starting to wonder about the Foundation again," said the leader of a women's project in the Caribbean.

The danger for the Foundation is that renewed pressure for conformity with administration policy could transform the concern about its future that now exists in the region into suspicion about its motives. "Everyone knows there has been a knock-down drag-out fight here," Fascell said. "But I don't think it has affected the grantees yet. Once it begins to affect them, to affect credibility, then the usefulness of the Foundation is gone."

The Foundation's survival has already exceeded the expectations of at least one of the original board members. "I felt from the beginning we'd have a ten-year free run," said Charles Meyer. "But I knew sooner or later the Foundation would become politicized. From the outset, I said that maybe we should self-destruct in ten years. Self-destruct and then reinvent the Foundation under a different name." Bill Dyal talked of the alternative of self-destruction as a weapon to defend the Foundation. "I believed the Foundation should have a self-destruct button built in," Dyal said. "We all believed that it would be better to let it die than to let it be distorted." Ultimately, the Foundation's future depends on the wisdom of its board of directors and their capacity to understand the vision behind Meyer's and Dyal's drastic prescriptions. Meyer, Dyal, and their colleagues consciously created a unique institution and knew that what was truly unique about it was something as fragile and easily lost as an attitude. The Foundation, they had decided, was to be responsive, but that entailed, not a series of procedures that could be institutionalized and made routine, but an attitude, a posture, a way people

A Prophetic Institution

could interact across national and cultural frontiers when they respected and trusted one another. For the Foundation, it meant a willingness to set sail with neither destination nor route determined beforehand.

The difficulties of understanding an institution which operates with that attitude go beyond the ideological views and political interests of any single administration. Many people are simply uncomfortable with that much openness. They want things to be more predictable. They want the illusion of being in control that the pursuit of a clearly defined goal gives. But if the Foundation succumbs to the temptation of greater control in the region, its uniqueness will vanish.

Even the best intentions and the most uncontroversial of goals, if set in Washington, would distort the Foundation. For example, at this writing, in the aftermath of political changes in Haiti and the Philippines, there is excitement in official Washington about what seems to be a running tide of democracy, particularly in Latin America and the Caribbean. The Foundation, some say, should play a more active role in encouraging that movement. But the question is, who defines democracy? Throughout its history, the Foundation has resisted going to the region with a preformed concept of democracy. Instead, it has demonstrated a willingness to support local manifestations of democratic values, even though they may differ in emphasis from U.S.-style democracy.

The challenge for the Foundation's board members is to be as open as their predecessors, to recognize that they are custodians, not so much of a small government bureaucracy, but of a fragile idea and a subtle web of human relationships. "What we need," said Congressman Fascell, "are broad minded, capable people to run the Foundation. That's not too much to ask. After all, these are presidential appointments."

Building Bridges

The distinction between short-term and long-term national interests is central to understanding the value of the Foundation to the United States. If a permanent objective of the United States is to build bridges to the people of other countries, then the Inter-American Foundation serves an important long-term interest. The Foundation's independence from the U.S. government has paid dividends for the United States by helping to communicate a more realistic picture of the diversity of its society. "Here in Argentina," said Roberto Martínez Nogueira, who has evaluated several Foundation projects, "it is common to have a monolithic image of the United States. It's either all good or all bad. The Foundation has contributed to a much more mature image."

Jorge Balán, director of CEDES, the social science research institution in Buenos Aires, echoed Martínez's words. "We've matured in Latin

Development and Dignity

America," he said. "In the 1970s, to accept aid from the U.S. government would bring immediate criticism. Now it's not so automatic. We've learned there are differences. In Argentina and other countries, academics and activists have changed their perspectives on the possibilities of cooperation with U.S. institutions. There's a more refined view of the United States and a greater understanding of its complexity and contradictions. This is especially true in the countries of the Southern Cone. These countries experienced military coups during the 1970s, which meant a political collapse, a sense of failure, a crisis of the politics practiced previously. They also experienced the crisis of Marxism, the intellectual system which had dominated discussion since the 1960s. The combination of a political crisis and a theoretical crisis led to confusions, contradictions, and a realization of how complex our own societies are. This contributed to a growing realization of the complexity of the United States."

Ironically, for many people in the region, an appreciation for the complexity of the United States came from witnessing the struggle over the Inter-American Foundation in recent years. To see the Foundation strive to maintain its independence in the midst of sweeping political and ideological changes in Washington and to see the various roles that members of Congress, the press, and public opinion played in that struggle was to see the U.S. political system at work. Because of the enduring strength of the early vision of the Foundation, it could steer a course of commitment to development in the region independent of changes in administration or outlook in Washington. "From the beginning," said Congressman Fascell, "we always felt the Foundation should never be politicized. We felt the concept behind it ought to be strong enough that it could withstand shifts in ideology."

By hewing to that course, the Foundation, small as it is, lends to relations between the United States and its neighbors in Latin America and the Caribbean a stability and continuity too often lacking. Those relations have typically been marred by a tendency on the part of the United States to veer between neglect and sudden concern. When no political threat is perceived in the region, the attention of U.S. policymakers wanes, in spite of the fact that social problems may be growing. Only when a threat to U.S. leadership is perceived do those problems come back into sharp focus. The Foundation, however, signifies a continuity of concern, rooted not in the short-term interests of any administration, but in the values of the people of the United States. "We always felt in our conversations with the Foundation," said Cardinal Raúl Silva Henríquez of Chile, "that we were in contact with the North American people, and not with the government that happened to be in power."

The value of that kind of relationship should be apparent to any intelligent analyst of long-term U.S. interests in the hemisphere.

Several observers have pointed out that 75 percent of the people of Latin America live in countries in which the Foundation is the only official U.S. agency active in development efforts. Moreover, because of its mandate to work with private groups, the Foundation is in direct contact with many of the most dynamic and creative people of the hemisphere. Finally, there is the observation that not all the dividends accruing to the United States are necessarily long-term. History sometimes moves with surprising speed, and even short-term interests are not immune from its sudden shifts. "Not too long ago," one Foundation staff member pointed out, "we were criticized for our projects in Chile. People in the administration said we were supporting the opposition. Then a wide spectrum of people signed the *Acuerdo,* a national platform for returning to democracy, and now our government is hailing the people who signed it, including some of the people we've worked with."

A Prophetic Institution

That the Inter-American Foundation has earned broad-based trust and even affection in Latin America and the Caribbean should be a cause of satisfaction to its creators, its officers and staff, and to the people of the United States whose taxes pay for it. That it should be regarded throughout the region as so unique should be a cause of concern. Latin Americans frequently call it *una organización insólita*—that is, unusual, unexpected. It's not what they expect from the United States. It's too good to be true. "It's a shame that Latin Americans have to call the Foundation 'una organización insólita,'" Bill Dyal said. "It's a shame that it's so unique in the U.S. government. The basic idea of the Foundation is that the people in Latin America and the Caribbean understand their problems better than we do. Why should that be so unique for us Americans?"

The trust and affection clearly do not arise from any perception that the Foundation is solving the region's development problems. The Foundation is a very modest enterprise. At its level of funding, its impact on the massive problems of poverty and underdevelopment is inevitably minimal. Its success seems connected to its operating style, but there is nothing particularly exotic about that, since it is based on traditional North American values of respect for the rights, opinions, and dignity of others, of extending a hand to a neighbor, and of admiring and supporting those who are willing to work hard on their own problems. "The basic theory is still sound," said Fascell. "You let people decide what they want to do, and you give them some help. And you never get very far away from that principle."

The Foundation's wide acceptance in the region has implications for aspects of relations between the United States and the Third

World, relations that in recent decades have seemed to bedevil U.S. policymakers. Perhaps the most comforting lesson from the Foundation's experiences is that the simple values most North Americans cherish, if put into practice with concern and respect, can produce a true partnership across frontiers. It was in that sense, said Peter Bell, that he concluded the Foundation was "a prophetic institution. It embodies and symbolizes the kinds of relationships with our neighbors that this country could—should—one day have."

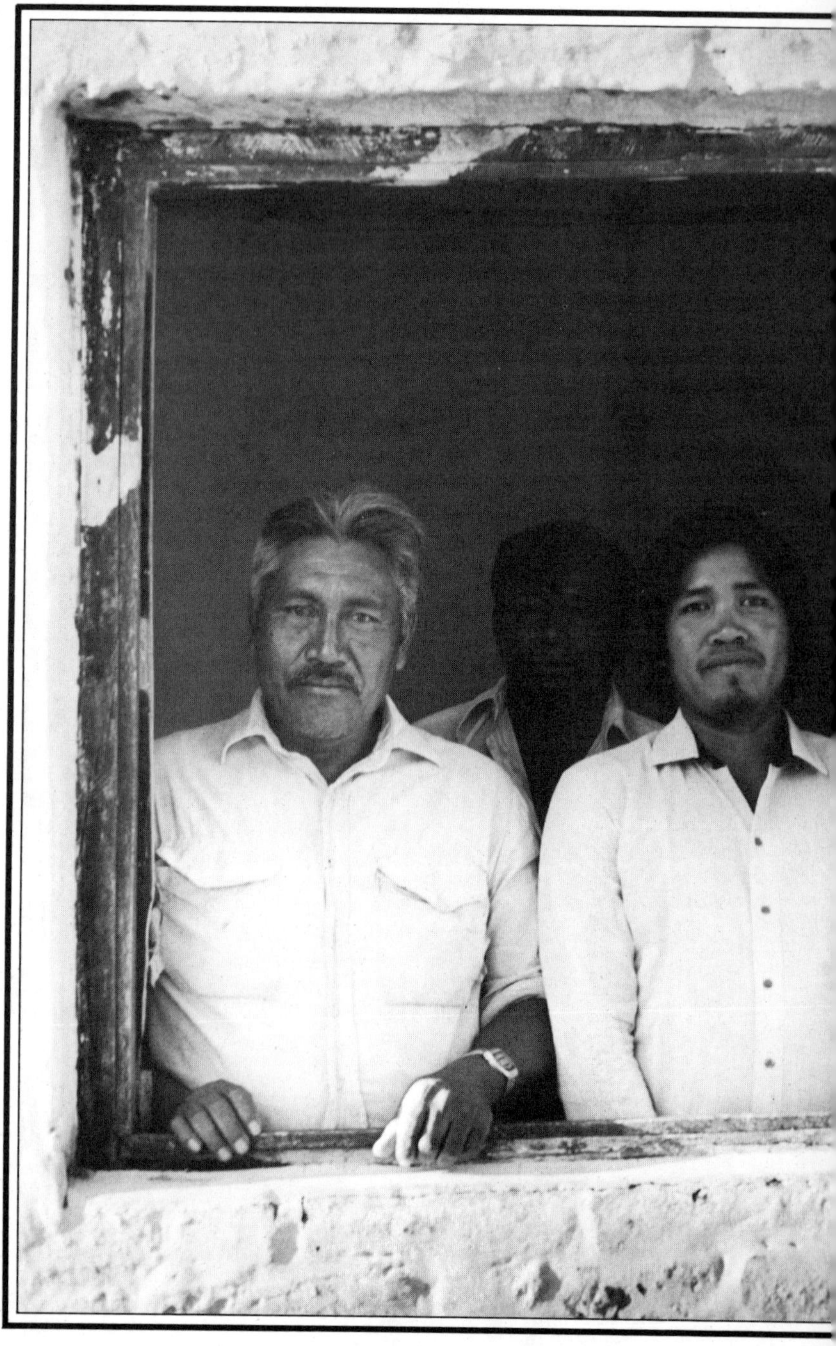

Development
and Dignity

Chapter 8

Chapter 8

Development and Dignity

"EL PATRÓN?" Narciso Severo repeated. He rolled the word on his tongue curiously, as if trying to identify some half-forgotten taste. "We don't use that word around here very much now," he finally said. Around him, seven other Paraguayan campesinos nodded. They were seated on light wooden chairs outside their general store in the rural community of Ciervo Cua Aribada, discussing the changes in their lives since they'd formed a cooperative. One of the most important, they agreed, was the change in their relationship with the owner of the store down the road—the man they once called "mi patrón." And as the word has faded gradually from the daily conversation of these campesinos, so too has a social institution that long held them in thrall.

Their cooperative is one of some fifty in the departments of Caazapá and Guairá, near the city of Villarrica, some 175 kilometers southeast of Asunción. Many of them benefit from an Inter-American Foundation grant provided to the Centro Paraguayo de Cooperativistas (CPC), a small, private, non-profit organization that promotes the spread of cooperatives among Paraguay's poorest peasants.

The CPC program sought to free peasants from their dependency on the patrón, the commercial middleman in the countryside. The peasant was bound to the patrón by a process seemingly as natural and implacable as the progression of the seasons. In the spring, he would buy seed and fertilizer from the patrón on credit. During the summer, he and his family would live on the goods purchased from the patrón's store, also on credit. By harvest season, the peasant was deeply in debt and obligated to sell his crop through the patrón. At each step of the process, the patrón set the prices and the peasant acquiesced. He had no choice.

The CPC used the Foundation grant for a fund from which the campesinos could draw the credit they needed to plant their crops and feed and clothe their families while they awaited the harvest. If they could get through the spring and summer without borrowing from the local patrón, they would not have to sell him their crops, but instead could look for the best price available. With loans from the fund, many communities set up small general stores carrying an assortment of basic necessities—flour, sugar, powdered milk, matches, canned food, cloth, tobacco, *yerba mate*, batteries for flashlights or radios, aspirin, and perhaps a few other medicines.

Development and Dignity

Bypassing the patrón, the peasants found they paid substantially less for their supplies and received substantially more for their crops. "Before, we didn't know what things cost," one said. "With the store, we see that the old patrón always marked up prices at least 20 percent, sometimes as much as 30 percent. We never received the market price for our crops. We would usually just get half that price." Severo summed it up: "Before, in the house of mi patrón, I bought dear and sold cheap. He helped us when we were in need, and in return we had to buy and sell with him. Now we buy what we need in our own store, where we know the scales are true. And when we sell, we know what the real prices are."

Throughout Latin America, the relationship between campesino and patrón has been the common structure of rural society. This exploitative relationship keeps campesinos in poverty and dependence, prevents them from ever getting ahead or even from making ends meet, and guarantees that they will be available as a cheap rural work force.

On the other hand, the relationship ameliorates to some extent the uncertainties and harshness of rural life. In an emergency, the campesino can appeal to the patrón for help—a loan to cover bills when a child is sick, for example. In extreme cases, the patrón, if he is willing to carry over debt, is the peasant's only protection against such catastrophes as crop failures. Although it is based on economics, the relationship may be complex, involving tradition, intertwined family histories, even affection. But it always involves dependency and deference and a cost to dignity. Now that they can rely on their own cooperative, none of the peasants in Ciervo Cua Aribada that day lamented its passing. "No longer do we have to go and beg the patrón for food or a bit of clothing on credit," said one.

A New Approach

Reaching poor people in communities like Ciervo Cua Aribada was the top priority for the congressmen who created the Inter-American Foundation and for the early board members and staff who shaped it. They wanted a new approach to economic and social development, one that would directly touch the lives of people whom previous attempts at development assistance couldn't seem to reach. Pursuing that goal, in the fifteen years since its creation, the Inter-American Foundation has spent about $220 million to support more than 2,000 projects in Latin America and the Caribbean. Over half that money—54 percent—came from the Social Progress Trust Fund, which receives repayments for Alliance for Progress loans made during the 1960s. The Foundation has access to a percentage of those repayments each year for support of projects in the country making

Development and Dignity

the repayments. The rest of its funds are appropriated yearly by the Congress. Those organizations receiving grants over the last fifteen years pledged contributions of time, energy, and financial resources averaging $1.23 to each Foundation dollar. Putting together taxpayers' dollars, loan repayments, and counterpart contributions, the Foundation has helped generate over half a billion dollars in resources for development in Latin America and the Caribbean in its fifteen years.

But the Foundation's role in development is conveyed less by numbers than by how it went about its task. A look at how its assistance reached Ciervo Cua Aribada brings into focus what was new about the Foundation's approach, how it has evolved, and where it now seems headed.

From the beginning there was debate within the Foundation over how best to reach the poor. Should the aid be channeled to base groups directly through funding discrete projects throughout the region, usually at the community level? Or should aid go to intermediary organizations that might be able to multiply the impact of the Foundation's funding through their contact with base groups? In practice, the Foundation has done both. But the bulk of its funding has gone through intermediaries. Thus, the Foundation's money did not go straight to Ciervo Cua Aribada. Instead, the Foundation approved a request for a grant from the CPC, a small intermediary group of Paraguayans with several years of experience in development work.

Requests, whether from intermediary or grassroots groups, usually come to the Foundation in a letter outlining the proposed project's beneficiaries, its goals, how they would be achieved, and how much money is needed. The letters range from the simple to the sophisticated. Bill Dyal often tells of an early request from a grassroots group in Belize written on brown wrapping paper. If the idea sounds good, the Foundation requests more specific information on the group making the proposal—its legal status, track record, sources of financing, staff—as well as further details on the project. The Foundation representative will check out the information provided and schedule a field visit. If the Foundation decides to fund, after a review process which usually brings in other representatives and staff members, a formal agreement is signed with the grantee. It specifies the activities to be carried out, the timetable, and the required narrative and financial reports, including audits.

Emerging Activists

Like many of the people described in previous chapters, the members of the CPC were educated professionals committed to working with the poor. Active in development work since the early 1960s, they had seen various efforts fail to make a dent in rural poverty. They had come to understand how poverty was maintained by social structures like the patrón relationship. Their experiences convinced them that change in such relationships was a prerequisite for development and that participation by the peasant was the key to success. "The problems we're talking about are the peasants' problems, not ours," said Miguel Angel Verdecchia, a founder of the CPC, in his solidly middle-class home in Asunción. "It's no good for us to drop in like parachutists to try to solve some problem. We don't live there. We can help them develop an organization that they can manage, and we can help transmit resources to them. But the people have to be involved in solving their own problems."

The appearance of committed private citizens like Verdecchia was a new phenomenon for most of the countries of the region. In a tradition that can be traced to colonial days and in a few cases even farther back to the hierarchial Indian empires toppled by the European conquest, the central state has always been the dominant institution. Early in the nineteenth century, many Latin American nations suffered bitter internal struggles between the forces of federalism, emphasizing regional autonomy, and the generally successful movement towards centralism and a unitary state. In this century, as middle-class and working-class groups emerged from the shadow of the traditionally dominant oligarchy, their struggle was carried on in the political arena and the goal was control of state power.

After World War II, the clamor for the solution of massive social problems grew louder, and the struggle for control of the state intensified. As a result, many of the nations of the region have been shaken by violent political oscillations. Aspiring dictators, conservative, centrist, reformist, and socialist political parties, right-wing and left-wing military factions, and guerrilla revolutionaries vied for power. Reactionaries, reformers, or radicals all saw control of the state as the necessary first step in putting their particular projects into practice.

Out of this turmoil, private initiatives emerged in every corner of the region. People began to discard the view that the national government was the necessary locus of all power and initiative. Some of those initiatives arose within community groups seeking solutions to local needs—a building for a community center, for example, or a water system. Some came from members of religious communities, expressions of the Catholic Church's "preferential option for the poor" or of increasing social activism within other churches. Some sprang from the example of social change in other countries; some from failed or frustrated government reforms. Many of these initiatives took the form of intermediary organizations, typically a group of professionals joining together to contribute their skills to development

Development and Dignity

efforts in several grassroots communities. Often, these professionals were motivated by coming in contact with poor people anxious to work on solving their own problems but lacking technical and organizational skills and money.

The architects who formed CECA in Colombia were one example. Patricio Wills of CECA recalled that he first became interested in development work through "the experience of finding people who weren't waiting for the government to help them but were doing something for themselves." In such initiatives, Wills saw the possibility of a way out of what, for him, is Colombia's central problem. "Paternalism is what's wrong with Colombian politics," he said. "Housing especially is central to politics. A housing project is the way the government has of giving favors. But this paternalism, the idea that the government will do everything for you, is corrupting, and it contributes to the political differences, to the mindless political strife here, to the violence. We find that the political differences disappear when the people are engaged in a project."

Carlos Morales, the professor who helped inspire Wills and his colleagues, has seen development efforts from both inside and outside the government. From 1972 to 1974, he was director of Acción Comunal y Asuntos Indígenas, Colombia's national agency for Community Development and Indian Affairs. "When I was director, I thought I could do a lot, but I found there were so many bureaucratic and political considerations that I couldn't do anything. So, I decided I'd had it with the government, after experiences like having to take up a collection in the office to buy medicines when there was an outbreak of measles around Santa Marta. Or when we needed to use some mules, and the bureaucracy wouldn't pay for the grass they ate until I reclassified it as 'fuel.'"

In Peru, various experiments in government-encouraged social change came to an end with the demise of the reformist military regime of General Juan Velasco Alvarado (1968–1975). Bereft of government resources and support, many of the people who had staffed those experiments eventually created intermediary organizations to continue working for social and economic development. "There are three hundred intermediary organizations working on development issues in Peru today," said Luis Soberón, who is a director of Antisuyo, a Foundation-backed marketing project seeking to protect the artisanal traditions of Peru's Indian peoples. "There's a historical coincidence between the existence of these groups and the interest on the part of foreign agencies like the Foundation in funding private development projects. This funding makes the people in these groups independent of the political and economic control of the government."

In Chile, where a repressive military government dismantled most of the social development efforts of previous civilian governments,

Development and Dignity

private and church-supported initiatives have multiplied. Many professionals and academics who were forced out of their positions or left because conditions were becoming intolerable have discovered ways to pursue their interests and their social commitments outside the government structure. "We were so focused on the state before," said Rodrigo Egaña of the Programa de Economía del Trabajo (PET), a private, non-profit research organization that works with the tiny businesses begun by many poor people in recent years. "I think all this experience will have a democratizing impact on Chile. We've learned that initiatives can be taken without the state, that even with the state totally opposed, things can be done. We've seen that one can live and do things without being a political officeholder. And I think agencies like the Inter-American Foundation must feel themselves a part of this process. They have transmitted some of those values having to do with private initiative that are common in the countries of the north."

Whatever the pattern in the region, the result has been what Albert O. Hirschman, in *Getting Ahead Collectively*, a book about several Foundation-supported projects, called "an impressive, loosely integrated network of national and international organizations which, at the level of any single Latin American country, performs important functions of education, public health, housing improvement, agricultural extension, development promotion of handicraft and small business."

For fifteen years now, the Foundation has been closely allied with many of the key organizations in this network. The support it has given to strengthen them is perhaps its most enduring contribution. "The problem in societies such as ours," said Ronnie Thwaites, who helped introduce legal services for the poor in Jamaica, "is to found stable institutions and give them strong roots in a brief period of time. The Foundation allowed us to graduate from being a good idea, run by do-gooders, into a settled institution for the service of poor people in this society."

Shared Values

These intermediary organizations tend to share, not only a new commitment to private involvement in solving social problems, but a common attitude that human growth and dignity are the main goals of the development process. Like all development agencies, they seek concrete changes for the better in the lives of the people they work with. In Paraguay, the CPC project has led to the increased use of machinery among campesinos who have joined cooperatives and to new profit-making activities. "Before we ground manioc by hand," said one campesino. "We beat corn with a stick. Now we

Development and Dignity

have proper machinery." Before the cooperative formed, said another, "we didn't even have an axe. Now we have a power saw that everyone can use." In one locality, the campesinos bought a motor for a sawmill on credit. "We wanted to make some use of the wood that was wasted when we cleared the forest for planting," a cooperative member explained. Another cooperative borrowed to buy equipment for a small sugar mill. "We plan to grow a lot of sugar cane," a member said. "We're better off if we can process the crops ourselves. There's a market for sugar cane syrup."

To be meaningful, most of these intermediary organizations believe, such concrete economic changes must go hand in hand with deeper changes. Their projects invariably emphasize democracy, participation, equality, responsibility, and personal growth toward a more dignified and fully human life. "You have to start by forming human beings," said Father Yvon Joseph, who runs a training program for development workers recruited from Haiti's impoverished countryside. "All the economic and social and political and spiritual processes come afterwards. Until the people feel human, nothing else is possible."

Because the projects of these intermediary groups so often aim at reinforcing dignity and self-confidence, they typically are based on the people's own values and cultural traditions. Many development projects ignore cultural considerations or drown them without a thought, like hydroelectric dams that flood hallowed ground. If they take the recipients' culture into account, it is often with the idea that it is a brake on development, an obstacle that must be replaced by superior cultural values—invariably those of the outsider proffering assistance. Throughout its history, the Foundation has taken a different view of the relationship between culture and development, one it shares with many of the intermediary organizations it has supported. Local cultural values are seen—not as obstacles—but as a necessary ingredient of successful development efforts. This attitude is not restricted to projects specifically aimed at preserving or strengthening local cultural expression, but pervades the whole range of Foundation-supported projects.

The CPC for example, consciously links formation of cooperatives in rural Paraguay to the tradition of the *minga*, the pattern of communal work that traces back to the Indian cultures and has persisted in many areas, although it is beginning to fade as cash crops replace subsistence agriculture. Rather than introducing an unfamiliar new structure, the CPC was building on the experiences and traditions of the peasants themselves.

Working with Intermediaries

Part of what was new about the Foundation's approach was that it sought out emerging intermediary institutions and supported them.

Development and Dignity

Also new was the collaborative style it evolved for working with them. The people who staff these intermediary organizations throughout Latin America and the Caribbean are among those who know the Foundation best. Because many of them also come in close contact with other development agencies, both official and private, they have a basis of comparison. In general, they tend to give the Foundation the highest marks for its ability to handle the always delicate relationship between donor and recipient.

"The whole question of a donation from an institution to a group of people is inherently an unequal relationship," said Luis Soberón in Lima. "You can't get away completely from the inequality, but you can work to make the relationship more horizontal." The Foundation has been able to work toward that goal largely because from the beginning it was structured to be responsive. It forgoes much of the apparatus considered essential by other development agencies. Originally authorized to have one hundred employees, it has operated for fifteen years with two-thirds that number. The current staff level is still only sixty-seven. The Foundation has no planning office, no warren of technical offices staffed by experts. Its organizational chart is a model of simplicity. There are the usual offices required for internal management of any bureaucracy. But the expressed work of the Foundation—to fund private groups engaged in development efforts—is carried out by representatives backed by a support staff. There is a coordinating level above the representatives, and then the Foundation's president.

The representatives have traditionally been dedicated to the Foundation's work in the countries for which they are responsible and do not see their assignment as only a step on the way up the bureaucratic ladder. "This place doesn't have the career orientation that the State Department does, for example," one representative said. "Rather, for most of the representatives, there is a commitment to a country, and that's shown in the attention to language and in cultural sensitivity."

People in the region agree. In Uruguay, Raúl Bidart of IPRU said, "I never had the sense with anyone from the Foundation that I was being used, as I've had with people from other institutions. I never had the feeling that they were interested in how the project could advance their careers." Alvaro Villa, who has known the Foundation since its first days in Colombia, said, "I have always been impressed by the quality of the staff and their command of the language. They speak perfect Spanish and are also interested in the culture. Each one is different; they're not like a regiment. But what is common to all is sensitivity."

The absence of policy planners and technical experts also implies that the Foundation does not have all the answers to development questions. "In my nine years here, I didn't find the answers," Bill

Dyal told the Foundation staff during a return visit. "And I would worry very much if you thought you had."

This means that the answers have to come from the region. The Foundation's role is to respond to initiatives from the region, proposals that grow out of local imagination, energy, and commitment to meet local needs. Its support allows local people to expand their activities, to survive a crisis, or to try a new direction. "The Foundation is not the push that gets you going," said Gustavo Herrera, a Colombian campesino organizer, "but the push that keeps you going."

Responsiveness, however, does not mean passivity. Gloria Torres, who runs a recreation program for children in Santiago, Chile, said, "The Foundation has high standards of efficiency. The representative questions closely and looks for concrete results. She pushes us. It's not at all an impersonal relationship. It's affectionate, a relationship of ideas, of sharing opinions. You have a different relationship with the Foundation than with other agencies, whose people you don't know. You can openly discuss your doubts with Foundation representatives. You feel you're developing the project together." In Quito, Ecuador, Padre Pio Baschirroto described the Foundation's representatives as "persons concerned for the preservation of local values, concerned that projects are not paternalistic but rather are ones that march toward independence for the groups. They are really concerned for the people who are supposed to be the beneficiaries of the projects."

"What we find interesting about the Foundation," said Chilean architect Eduardo Walker, "is that they question us to make our work more rigorous. The representatives have always been interested in the impact of our work on the people in the *poblaciones* and want to make sure that the benefits actually reach them. Yet they don't impose values on us, although they share certain values and beliefs with us. You don't have to explain everything to them. They're experienced in the concepts we're talking about."

In Haiti, Father Yvon Joseph described the relationship between the Foundation and his organization, which trains *animateurs* for work in rural areas, as "very much like the relations we have with the people we work with. It's a listening, learning relationship, there's much talking, discussing—an interest we don't always find in other institutions. Some institutions only want reports. With the Foundation, it's more a question of working together to find the best things for the people."

Respect for the grantees is axiomatic in this approach. "Most of our grantees don't see themselves as recipients of foreign aid," one representative said. "They're comfortable with the fact that we don't have a larger agenda for them." In Jamaica, Ronnie Thwaites agreed. "It is easy for aid to be oppressive," he said, "to squash what you

Development and Dignity

think of yourselves. The Foundation never imposed itself after that fashion. It was never a handout, and never a veiled big-stick relationship. It was people with a particular resource willing to help people with a particular idea."

A Pilot Fish?

Those who created the Inter-American Foundation realized that its resources alone would not have any major impact on the hemisphere's development needs. The Foundation spent under $27 million last year, less than one-half of one percent of the U.S. foreign assistance budget. But they also knew that efforts such as the Alliance for Progress, with its billions of dollars, had fallen far short of the hopes it raised. Perhaps something more modest but innovative might work: a pilot fish of a program instead of a whale.

The Foundation, Congressman Dante Fascell said during hearings in 1972, was meant to be "a small-scale program designed to develop innovative techniques that would, in turn, lead to further understanding of this complex field and eventually to a speeding up of the process of social development throughout the hemisphere." He urged Foundation officals to disseminate experience quickly. "It is extremely essential that when you have a successful project you immediately get the word out to Congress, to the executive, and to other people in the social development field and in the academic community."

So if the Foundation's first mandate was to get assistance to the poor, the second was to learn from its experience and communicate the lessons to others interested in development. That second mandate has preoccupied and bedeviled the Foundation from the beginning. In the early days, there was a debate between those who argued that the Foundation's function was simply to fund and those who maintained that the only reason for funding was to learn. The first position, pushed to an extreme, became known as the "Harley-Davidson approach." It evoked the image of a Foundation representative riding up to a project, dropping off a bag of money, and disappearing into the sunset, never to return. The image on the opposite extreme was of a neat scientific framework, a laboratory, in which projects would exist simply to test hypotheses about development.

In practice, the Foundation eschewed the pretense that it was engaged in pure science, but the image of the laboratory was never laid to rest. It reappears periodically, tied to the idea that other institutions in the international development community are the primary audience for what the Foundation learns about development. Of course, the image of the Foundation as a laboratory, with its suggestion of scientific precision, is incompatible with the Foundation's method of operation. Scientists work in laboratories so that they can control experiments and limit the number of variables involved. The Foundation works in the real world, the "experiments" are designed by others, and the number of variables can be infinite. But the "laboratory" image raises expectations that the Foundation can deliver succinct formulas that other development agencies could promptly employ.

Seeking a more modest model for their efforts to learn about development and communicate that knowledge, Foundation staff turned to the idea of funding "replicable" projects, those that if successful in one setting might serve as models in another. Gradually, they came to see this approach as somewhat mechanistic as well. Different settings were by definition different. Touting something that had worked in one place might distort in another the process of people finding their own solutions. Again, the question arose: Just who was supposed to be learning: Development professionals? Academics? The general public? The grantees?

The answers have varied in emphasis over the years, and efforts have been made periodically to communicate the Foundation's experiences to outside audiences in some systematic way. The Foundation has published several books and monographs on development issues that, like its journal, *Grassroots Development*, draw on and analyze project experiences. The most ambitious of these was a survey of all 305 projects funded in the first five years, which led to the publication of *They Know How*, the first comprehensive statement of the Foundation's approach to development.

"That book came out of an intuitive approach," said George Evans, Peace Corps director in Costa Rica and a Foundation staff member during the early years. "We told the representatives to pick the projects they thought were doing well and the ones that were doing poorly. We looked at what characteristics each group had in common. That led to the ideas about vital signs and social gains."

Ninety-four projects were analyzed in depth. The result was a more precise description of what the Foundation and the groups that it had supported were pursuing. Practically all development efforts pay at least lip service to the idea that the alleged beneficiaries should participate in projects. Through analysis of successes and failures, the Foundation was able to break that concept down into a search for specific behaviors, processes, mechanisms, and outcomes—the "vital signs"—that more clearly defined participation and indicated whether it was occurring. That way of looking at a group, or at the relationship between an intermediary group and the grassroots, became the heart of the Foundation's decision-making process on whether or not to fund any given project.

Most of the vital signs could be measured by questions about the degree of control beneficiaries exercised over a project and their critical understanding of a project's implications. Did they voice their demands and desires before the project began? Is there a structure that permits them to do so during the course of the project? Does formal control increasingly pass to the beneficiaries? Can they decide on how project resources are allocated? Is the project dependent on the good will of outsiders or the leadership of a single individual? Could it continue in the face of adversity or when the leadership changes? Was momentum already present before the project was funded, that is, were the participants already embarked on their efforts, or is the project simply a response to the possibility of funding? What criteria have been set for sharing the benefits of the project, and are the criteria those of the beneficiaries themselves? Do they understand the implications for themselves of decisions about financing, indebtedness, and types of technology? Do they understand the sacrifices they are undertaking and the economic, social, and political risks they may be running?

They Know How also laid out more detailed ways to discuss the outcomes of projects. Most development projects aim at improvements in standards of living—better diet and health, potable water, upgraded housing, more income and education—which can be measured fairly easily. But most also make claims in the less precise area of social change. Given its congressional mandate to concentrate on that area, the Foundation developed indicators—"social gains"—that more clearly described whether such change was in fact occurring. Social gains included changes in the beneficiaries' relationships with other institutions and other people in their societies: more access to needed resources, more leverage through collective strength, a wider range of choices, legitimation when their cause is recognized as valid by others. Social gains also included subjective changes in the beneficiaries: increased capability for critical reflection, increased discipline to accept and complete individual and collective tasks, and an increasing orientation toward the future and toward postponing immediate gratification for possibly greater benefits.

The production of *They Know How* was a major effort that took much of the Foundation's energy for the better part of a year. Once the book was done, the staff turned back to the work of funding. The imperative to justify itself to policymakers and to the rest of the development community diminished for a time. But learning as a central activity of the Foundation continued. The staff continued to learn from experience with projects and to apply that learning to their decisions about new projects. And the grantees, both intermediary and grassroots groups, learned as well. Despite the cyclical pressure to communicate lessons to a perceived audience of other development agencies, the idea that the grantees should be the principal learners remained a constant for the Foundation. While it experimented with various ways of disseminating information about the projects it supported to broader audiences, the Foundation continued to facilitate conferences and visits to bring together grantees with shared interests from neighboring provinces or from distant countries.

"It was not only the financial support from the Foundation that was valuable," said Fabio Londoño, director of the legal services program for peasants around Cali, Colombia. "It was the possibility of exchanging experiences with other groups in Latin America working in the juridical field, the chance to participate in seminars with people from other groups."

"The opportunity to go to Bogotá to look at projects that were preserving traditional handicrafts was very important for us," said Carolyn Heath in Lima. Heath works with Antisuyo, the organization that seeks to protect the traditional handicrafts of the Indian peoples of Peru.

A striking example of the value of this kind of cross-fertilization can be found in Puerto Plata, a frequent port of call for tourist cruise ships on the Dominican Republic's north coast. The appearance of hundreds of tourists on shopping sprees with coins jingling in their pockets spawned a horde of begging and insistent street kids. Tourists complained, the cruise ship operators threatened to bypass Puerto Plata, and local authorities responded by rounding up the kids with nightsticks and penning them up in an open yard under the midday Caribbean sun until the tourists cast off.

"It pains me to see people suffer," said Ana Leroux, a public spirited grandmother who ran a dress shop in Puerto Plata. "I was desperate seeing the children beaten and mistreated. I got some friends together and we formed a committee to do something about it. Soon after, I met someone from the Foundation who told me about the program for gamins in Bogotá. One of the priests who worked with the gamins, Father Irenarco Ardila, was in the States. The Foundation arranged for him to stop here on his way back to Colombia. He spent eleven days with us, explaining to us all about their program and helping us organize our program here."

Setting the Research Agenda

The Foundation emphasizes direct learning from experience with its projects, but it also provides support for independent study of development issues. In mid-1973, it began to offer fellowships to doctoral candidates in U.S. universities who were interested in studying social change. The purpose was to encourage a more problem-oriented and multidisciplinary approach in research on social change in Latin America and the Caribbean and especially to increase the focus on grassroots processes and on poor people. "We felt a tremendous need to put future Latin American and Caribbean experts in touch with the grantees," said Bill Dyal. "It was important to get their sights down to what was important."

The program began modestly—four fellows were selected in 1974, six the following year. Later, it was expanded to master's candidates as well and to students from Latin America and the Caribbean. So far, a total of 402 fellowships have been awarded, 164 to candidates for master's degrees, 174 for doctorates, 8 at the post-doctoral level, and 64 to candidates from Latin America and the Caribbean. The largest number of research topics—169—has been in the area of agricultural and rural development. Other popular areas have been urban small enterprises, education and training programs, and community services, including health and legal assistance.

"It was a healthy mix of theoretical rigor and practicality," one former fellow said. "Plenty of institutions fund scholarly work, but they shy away from work with a practical relevance. The Inter-American Foundation looks at both sides by examining the theoretical implications of a practical problem with which they are involved."

"The Foundation fellowship," said another former fellow, "encourages research as if people mattered. By that I mean it looks at problems that are important to people at the grassroots level. I remember sensing that some of the representatives were critical of the fellowship program. I think they felt it was not a good use of money. They have low overhead costs, and they want their money to go to projects in the field. I think the fellowship is important, but I understood their views. It made me more conscious of my responsibility in using those funds to provide something the people in the region could use."

In addition to the fellowship program, which supports research in the field, the Foundation has provided both short- and long-term internships permitting young people to learn about development through work in the Foundation's office. Many of those interns later move on to other agencies active in development work, taking with them a unique perspective. "I used to think about Latin America and the Caribbean in terms of their development needs for improved food production, better educational systems, and modern technology, material, and planning," said Alex Palacios, a former Foundation intern who went to the Peace Corps and later to the U.S. Committee for UNICEF. "But I learned to think about development in terms of what already exists—the institutions, the organizations, the emerging leaders, and how to help them."

Linking Research and Action

Ever since the presidency of Peter Bell, the Foundation has actively supported local research institutions seeking knowledge about the development process. Especially in the Southern Cone countries, the Foundation learned how to blend its interest in ideas that might help poor people with the interest of social scientists in research. Many established institutions were starting to explore new directions, to put more emphasis on reaching people at the bottom. This was in line with the Foundation's mandate, and the Foundation was at times able to support and encourage these new directions.

The Foundation has always been an activist organization. It believes in jumping in and doing something, and then learning from the experience. But while always intensely learning, during its early years the Foundation was reluctant to fund research projects. However, during the mid-1970s, that reluctance came into conflict with the impulse to support some of the academic groups coming under pressure from violent and repressive military governments. The Foundation searched for ways to help that linked research to action on poverty. Meanwhile, local researchers were exploring the limits of relevant investigation possible under military regimes. Gradually, new links were forged between academics and the people at the bottom of their societies. New styles of work and new research interests evolved. Many of the people closest to the process believe that the changes are lasting.

"The Foundation always had a great interest in learning," said Roberto Martínez Nogueira in Argentina, "and that has enabled some people in the social sciences to emerge both from the ivory tower and from the corner into which the events of recent years had driven them. The Foundation has had an impact on the work of social scientists."

Elizabeth Jelin of CEDES in Buenos Aires agreed. "The demands of the Inter-American Foundation and other institutions forced us out of the traditional framework of academic research." She mentioned examples from some of the work done in recent years at CEDES. "We did a lot of work with people in poor neighborhoods, trying to see how they were affected by changes in Argentina and how they responded to those changes. But it was a special kind of investigation, with a great deal of feedback from the participants. We were trying to see them as subjects, not objects, people creating their own reality, a different view than traditional social science. At the moment, we're finishing a book of photographs, which were chosen by the people of the barrio. The photographs were shot by a professional photographer, then submitted to the people for their criticisms and opinions. Some of those will be included in the book. We tried to get at their view of their barrio and of themselves, through the images they chose and the words they used to explain their choices. You know, after doing this kind of work, you can never go back to the traditional social science research."

In Chile, Rodrigo Egaña of the Programa de Economía del Trabajo (PET) described a similar process. With a Foundation grant, PET began to study the "informal sector" in Santiago, the tiny businesses formed by poor people as a means of subsistence in a military-run economy that ignored them. "We did the first study of that sector. And soon, since we were the only institution these poor business owners knew, they began to ask us for advice. This led to a discussion within PET on what to do next, how to respond. Faced with the problems of half a million people, we couldn't say we were just researchers. We realized we couldn't respond to the overall problem, so we concentrated on training the emerging leaders of the groups that these people were forming to help them deal with problems. So we've become almost like a consulting firm for these groups. And we've learned that our work as professionals, as researchers, has to be linked to providing some solutions to the problems these people are facing. We have to be involved with them. Now a lot of academics here seem to be doing this kind of applied research involving a lot of feedback with community groups and organizations.

"All this experience has engendered a new style of work, defined by values and by the goals of the research, rather than by any particular methodology. The only methodology to which we're wedded is refusing to use the groups like lab animals. And these new styles of work are very attractive. When change comes here, when the universities are free again, I don't think they'll disappear."

Looking Around and Looking Ahead

In its fifteenth year, the staff of the Inter-American Foundation could look back on many solid achievements. The Foundation had earned the trust of people throughout the region. It had contributed significantly to an expanding movement of initiatives by private citizens at work on the social problems of their nations. In the most remote corners of the hemisphere, its funds were helping groups of people realize some of their dreams of a better life for their families. Because of its close contact with people at the grassroots, it had a better insight into what was happening there than most other development agencies. "When I was at the Foundation," said Peter Bell, "I felt I was seeing Latin America from the inside."

But a look around would also reveal several problems. Not all projects had prospered. Many of the more ambitious projects of the early years, particularly the worker-managed enterprises, had collapsed. Smaller projects often faltered and then failed because the beneficiaries lacked the technical skills to carry them through. As the Foundation's portfolio grew, it became increasingly difficult for the representatives to keep in touch with projects they had funded. "The representatives each investigate about twenty projects a year," current President Deborah Szekely pointed out, "and fund about half of them. But they have another thirty on-going projects." The quarterly month-long visits to the field typical for Foundation representatives became more and more endurance contests run at breakneck speed.

As the pressures on representatives and support staff increased, the possibilities for learning lessons from the projects diminished and the job of communicating those lessons to others was farmed out to consultants. Many project records were incomplete long after the funding had ended; project histories went unwritten. A wealth of experience was being accumulated about hundreds of the most varied kinds of development projects, but not enough of it was being captured and passed on to others who could use it.

At the same time, changes were taking place that presented new obstacles to development and new challenges to the Foundation. The debt crisis threatened to overwhelm many of the countries in which the Foundation had been active. Budget pressures in the United States meant shrinking sums for development assistance. The Foundation's budget was cut three times between 1980 and 1985. Cynicism and disillusion with foreign aid were on the increase in the United States. Domestic political pressures on the Foundation fed perceptions in the region that it was becoming more cautious, more fearful of making mistakes, more interested in projects than process, and less independent of U.S. government policy.

"I've noticed a change of attitude," said Rene Rodriguez, one of the key figures in the ill-fated worker self-management movement in Peru. "From 1976 to 1980 or 1981, the Foundation was supporting a process. There was something in common in all its projects, a process of structural change, based on the organized poor. Now the Foundation is doing assistance. Small is beautiful. I don't see the repeatability of the projects. Why the change? I imagine political pressures."

Meanwhile, many of the groups with which the Foundation had worked were changing as well. Both intermediary and grassroots groups had become more experienced and sophisticated about development. Many intermediary organizations were receiving funding from a number of both official and private sources in Europe and Canada as well as the United States. In many cases, the poor had become more organized and knowledgeable about the self-help development process.

A Changing Foundation

The Foundation has also changed over the years. The ways it responds to the groups with which it works evolved as its guiding concepts were continuously refined by experience. *They Know How*, the book that is virtually a bible for the Foundation, argues adamantly that the people closest to the problem know best what they need for its solution. That idea still guides the Foundation's approach, but it has been modified by experience. "I've changed my mind," said George Evans. "We don't know everything, nor do they. *They Know How* was a strong statement, a necessarily strong statement to counter the typical assumptions about development, to counter the idea that all you needed to solve the problem was money and technology. But there are situations where the technical skills are just not there, and some outside intervention should come in."

A current staff member adds: "We have matured from touting the poor as the source of all knowledge. However, we do regard the best locus of the solution to be as close to the problem as possible, and hence we look first and foremost to talent in the host countries."

"In the early days," said Sal Pinzino, a former Foundation representative who later ran the Catholic Relief Services program in Bolivia, "we got around suspicions by proving that we were not interventionists. The projects were in the hands of the people themselves, and we were able to prove the trust we put in people. If we'd taken a stronger role, we might have avoided some of the negative consequences of our funding, but Dyal was willing to take that risk rather than lose the trust. Now the trust is there. The Foundation shouldn't sit back and let problems in a project grow. It must still be respectful, but it doesn't have to walk on eggshells anymore."

Responsiveness, another central tenet of the Foundation's faith, has also evolved over time. "We're not simply responsive," said one representative. "We're directive in our search for projects. We're not just throwing seed money into a field and seeing what sprouts. We're making little holes in certain areas of the field to plant the seeds in."

Many of the representatives have developed a "cluster" approach to funding. "Instead of taking responsiveness and randomness to their extreme, we're going for a critical mass in certain areas in certain countries," said one. "Everybody wants the big bang," said another. "But we have to think in terms of impact at the local and regional level, not at the national level. I look for regional opportunities where there's a cluster of possible projects."

"Our funding should be concentrated, targeted," another representative said. "We should concentrate on those activities or areas than can demonstate how a bottom-up process can grow into larger movements through organization and networking to significantly affect regions, and how partnerships between grassroots communities, private development agencies, government ministries, extension programs, and international development agencies can generate larger development momentum."

Ken Cole is director of the Small Projects Fund at the Inter-American Development Bank (IDB). It provides grants for technical assistance and loans to small organizations, frequently cooperatives, in Latin America and the Caribbean. "It's not uncommon that the Inter-American Foundation helps an organization build up a couple of steps," he said, "and then we can move in. We've done that in Panama, Honduras, and Guatemala. There are several cases in Uruguay where the Foundation has laid some groundwork and we came in later. Manos del Uruguay, for example, was the first such project we funded."

Manos is a network of groups of rural women who produce high quality clothing and decorative goods for the national and international market. Several women working as volunteers got it going in the late 1960s. By 1974, it had grown into a potentially significant employer of rural women. "Someone from the IDB approached us," said Olga Artagavetia, the president of Manos, "and we presented a project. But then I realized we weren't ready for what we were taking on. We didn't have the structure for the IDB project. And at that moment, the Foundation appeared. The representative sat with us to talk about what we needed and about how the Foundation could help. The unexpected thing was the speed with which the help came. That project provided us the training to improve our administrative structure. It lasted maybe six months, yet it was crucial to us. It helped us compete in a world where our competitors don't put, as we do, part of the profits back into education and training for our women. It also helped improve our organization. Later on when we were capable of handling their assistance we were able to go back to the IDB."

New Responses

The Foundation's major institutional response to problems in managing its expanding portfolio of projects and in drawing lessons about development from it, is a new approach to project monitoring that Deborah Szekely and board chairman Victor Blanco have encouraged. The Foundation is contracting development specialists within each country to visit and monitor projects on a regular schedule. One aim is more regular contact with projects than a single Foundation representative can provide. A report analyzing the Foundation's projects after the first five years contained the frank admission: "We do not really know what is happening in about one-third of the projects." The new monitoring systems are designed to change that. Through periodic reports on the projects, the monitors can keep the representative better informed and serve as a contact point so that bureaucratic or communications problems can be promptly resolved and needs for technical assistance promptly met.

"I think it leads to a better and more open relationship with the groups," said Roberto Jiménez, who is in charge of the system in Costa Rica. "We've introduced spread sheets in about thirty projects so far to help grantees keep track of costs, of check deposits, and so on. Before, the record-keeping system tended to be very confused, and accountants usually couldn't file complete reports. In addition, we have done analyses with certain groups that point up what is happening financially within the group and permit discussion of problems as soon as they show up. And by doing the initial processing of proposals here, we can help speed up the Foundation's response time. Often proposals don't contain all the information the Foundation needs to decide on a project and there are letters and phone calls back and forth and a lot of delay and frustration. With this system, we can resolve the problems here and send more complete data to the Foundation."

The increased grassroots contact that the monitoring systems promise and the more thorough reporting about on-going projects has encouraged the Foundation to experiment with mechanisms to make its funding more flexible in the future. For example, it is attempting to provide early support for emerging grassroots groups. Traditionally, a group's track record has been an important consideration in the Foundation's decision whether or not to fund it. New "in-country funds" now being set up will provide for "start-up" grants of up to $5,000 each year to emerging groups in need of some small piece of equipment, technical assistance, or training. "There's a 'moment of development,'" one Foundation staff member explained. "Development happens in the moment when a group of people recognize a problem or a need and decide to do something about it. We're trying to get closer to that moment, to be there with some support when it occurs." The in-country services systems should help the Foundation identify these emerging grassroots groups at an earlier stage in their growth, and permit close tracking of the impact on them of the start-up grants.

"Partnership grants" are a second experiment in funding that Szekely and Blanco are pushing. Most Foundation grants are short-term, one to three years, and tied to specific projects. "I always thought that was a little wooden," said Ronnie Thwaites in Jamaica. "The idea that everything had to be a three-year grant sometimes didn't fit the situation. Sometimes it was difficult for the Foundation to disengage. Friends were unmade in some cases, or dependency turned out to have actually increased. Perhaps what the Foundation has never done well is to end a relationship."

In an attempt to meet that problem, over the next few years, a limited number of longer-term grants for institutional support will go to organizations that already play an important development role in their societies but need an extended period of time to become self-sufficient. Many effective development organizations find themselves constantly hampered by the fact that funders prefer to support concrete projects rather than an organization's overhead. Often, such organizations are quite active in various projects, usually tailored to the interests of funders, while growing increasingly weaker at their core. By guaranteeing institutional support for an extended period of time, the partnership grants should permit these organizations more freedom to identify their goals and plan their strategies. Szekely also believes this extended grant period will give the groups an opportunity to develop their own infrastructure for local fundraising.

Monitoring and Learning

In addition to their potential for improving funding, the in-country systems have major implications for the Foundation's role in disseminating experience and information about development. With their regular contact with projects throughout a country, they can increase the amount of horizontal learning—among grassroots and intermediary groups—that the Foundation has always favored. "One of the things we can do is help spread technical experience and expertise from one project to another," said Bruno Podestá, who helps run the in-country monitoring system in Peru. From their exposure to a wide variety of projects and their regular reporting on processes within those projects, the monitors themselves should become increasingly knowledgeable about development. There is also the potential for increased publication on development issues within each country as monitors and other researchers mine the growing store of data on individual projects. In the not-too-distant future, the in-country systems could be seen as a valuable training ground for local development workers, much as the Peace Corps has been for the ranks of development specialists in the United States.

But perhaps the greatest learning potential of the in-country systems is that they might permit the Foundation to become what it has always aspired to be—a clearinghouse of knowledge about development. Regular reporting by the monitors will give the Foundation a richer body of information about development processes in concrete situations than it has ever had before. Ultimately, it should provide a more complete data base that researchers can tap to test development theories. It could make readily accessible to grassroots groups or intermediary organizations interested in a certain type of project the accumulated experience of others throughout the hemisphere. And through an expanded publications schedule it could provide the information base for more ambitious communication with a broader public about foreign assistance, development, and the economic, social, and political context within which development efforts are made.

Looking Ahead and Looking Back

Still more innovations are in the Foundation's future. Szekely and Blanco have already moved the Foundation toward a dramatic increase in support for small business ventures and productive activities in the cities and towns of the region. In 1985, nearly $13 million of over $22 million in Foundation grants—56 percent of the total portfolio—went to small enterprises including market women tending vegetable stalls or family businesses producing rustic furniture and handicrafts. In many of these projects local business elites provide technical assistance to small enterprises, thus forging links between themselves and their poor compatriots.

In another innovation, Szekely is encouraging the drawing up of "country plans" in collaboration with grantees and development specialists in each country to assure that the Foundation is responsive to local ideas. She plans eventually to support small centers that provide training in organizational skills and technical assistance for isolated rural communities. More funds will go to develop networks of local and intermediary groups at the regional and national levels. The Foundation's unique bottom-up perspective on the region will be exploited to identify and study trends that have implications for development. One example might be the shift throughout the region from traditional sharecropping or patrón-peon relationships to seasonal, salaried, urban-based agricultural labor. Another might be the emerging links between the protection of natural resources and ethnic groups, as in the case of the Kuna Indians; and between science, conservation, and development, as in a Foundation-supported experiment in Panama to raise iguanas in captivity to help improve rural diets. New ways of communicating the Foundation's development experiences are in preparation, including educational videos about specific projects.

All the innovations are designed to better carry out the mandates given the Foundation at its creation—to reach the poor people of the hemisphere and to communicate to others the lessons learned from that effort. During its first fifteen years, the Foundation earned an enviable position of trust throughout the region and garnered a rich store of development experience. Its commitment to the people with whom it works demands that it constantly strive to improve its effectiveness while contributing to an understanding of the development process. The challenge for the Foundation is to do so without losing sight of the original ideas and values that made it a unique (and *insólita*) institution.

In funding, that means providing more effective assistance to grassroots groups without altering the basic hands-off, responsive philosophy. Over the years, the Foundation has seen that timely

Development and Dignity

technical assistance often could have saved projects from crises or failure. But it has also seen that there are worse things than failure, and that out of the lessons of failure can come new and stronger initiatives.

In learning, it means organizing and more systematically using the increased information about development experiences now becoming available through the in-country monitoring systems, without falling victim to the illusion that increased information guarantees increased understanding.

Ultimately, it means remembering that development work remains more a matter of informed hunches based on experience and sensitivity than a science. Every project is in part a leap into the dark. Questions abound. The Foundation has always worked with the tension of ultimately unanswerable questions: Will the proposed project do more harm than good? Where is the line between supporting a project and directing it? What is the optimum relationship between an intermediary group and a grassroots project? There are no final answers to such questions. They must be asked in the context of every project as it comes up. That means the Foundation as an institution must maintain a posture of constant questioning, not only of those seeking its support, but also of itself.

Development, as the Foundation has practiced it, comes down, when all is said and done, to a gamble on people. A gamble that the desperately impoverished inhabitants of Chambrum in Haiti will have the energy and will to dig irrigation ditches when they see the possibility of getting water for their sunbaked fields. A gamble that Juan García's quest for the history and folklore of the black people of Ecuador will reinforce their sense of identity and of belonging. That a priest knows what he's doing when he proposes moving hundreds of Colombia's street kids to an isolated jungle. That young architects in several countries will maintain their commitment to the slum dwellers they've promised to help. That a team of rural organizers in Colombia or Paraguay will survive failure and frustration and help form a successful cooperative next time.

Those who created the Inter-American Foundation and put it into operation were eager to gamble on the people of the hemisphere. The experience of fifteen years teaches that their approach, wielded with care and sensitivity, is no longer a gamble. As Dante Fascell said in celebration of the Foundation's fifteenth anniversary, "The staff, officers, and members of the board of the Inter-American Foundation, past and present, gave people a chance, and they jumped in. No one pushed them. Their pride and their spirit of cooperation emerged because there wasn't some big brother, some great planner, telling them what to do. They took their own ideas for projects to improve their lives and made them happen."